Treasured

2017 Poetry Collection

Treasured represents our student authors as accurately as possible.
Every effort has been made to print each poem
as it was submitted with minimal editing
of spelling, grammar, and punctuation.
All submissions have been formatted to this compilation.

Copyright © 2017 by The America Library of Poetry
as a compilation.

Copyrights to individual poems belong to the authors.

All rights reserved.
No part of this book may be reproduced in any way
without the expressed written permission of the publisher.

Published by
The America Library of Poetry
P.O. Box 978
Houlton, ME 04730
Website: www.libraryofpoetry.com
Email: generalinquiries@libraryofpoetry.com

Printed in the United States of America.

**THE AMERICA
LIBRARY OF POETRY**

ISBN: 978-0-9966841-3-2

Contents

In Memory Of 4
Foreword 5
About the Editor's Choice Award 6
Spirit of Education Award 7

Poetry by Division

Division I
Grades 3-5 9

Division II
Grades 6-7 65

Division III
Grades 8-9 121

Division IV
Grades 10-12 159

Index of Authors 218

Ordering Treasured 223

Treasured

In memory of our student author,
Takoda Turner

Father Time
by Takoda Turner
(February 7, 1997 – January 14, 2017)
Poem written during 12th grade

Father Time is like Father Rhyme because they go at a certain pace
But they both agree that it is not a race
Both grow old and weary
But only Father Time has Baby New Yeary
In all of Father Time's success
He has no time to possess
For Baby New Year who is supposed to have more success
Than the past fathers of time

Foreword

There are two kinds of writers in the world.
There are those who write from experience,
and those who write from imagination.
The experienced, offer words that are a reflection of their lives.
The triumphs they have enjoyed, the heartaches they have endured;
all the things that have made them who they are,
they graciously share with us, as a way of sharing themselves,
and in doing so, give us, as readers, someone to whom we may relate,
as well as fresh new perspectives
on what may be our common circumstances in life.
From the imaginative,
come all the wonderful things we have yet to experience;
from sights unseen, to sounds unheard.
They encourage us to explore the limitless possibilities
of our dreams and fantasies,
and aid us in escaping, if only temporarily,
the confines of reality and the rules of society.
To each, we owe a debt of gratitude;
and rightfully so, as each provides a service of equal importance.
Yet, without the other, neither can be truly beneficial.
For instance, one may succeed in accumulating a lifetime of experience,
only to consider it all to have been predictable and unfulfilling,
if denied the chance to chase a dream or two along the way.
Just as those whose imaginations run away with them never to return,
may find that without solid footing in the real world,
life in fantasyland is empty.
As you now embark, dear reader,
upon your journey through these words to remember,
you are about to be treated to both heartfelt tales of experience,
and captivating adventures of imagination.
It is our pleasure to present them for your enjoyment.
To our many authors,
who so proudly represent the two kinds of writers in the world,
we dedicate this book, and offer our sincere thanks;
for now, possibly more than ever,
the world needs you both.

Paul Wilson Charles
Editor

Editor's Choice Award

The Editor's Choice Award is presented
to an author who demonstrates not only
the solid fundamentals of creative writing,
but also the ability to elicit an emotional response
or provide a thought provoking body of work
in a manner which is both clear and concise.

You will find "August"
by Anushka Shah on page 217 of Treasured

2017
Spirit of Education
For Outstanding Participation

Ernest Becker
Middle School

Las Vegas,
Nevada

Presented to participating students and faculty
in recognition of your commitment
to literary excellence.

Division 1

Grades 3-5

Pets Are Great
by Gabe Monson

Pets are great
they love to play
they love to greet
and they lay all day
My dogs are small
they come when I call
they don't like cats
roaming around the house
they love to play
they love to lay
sometimes they sit around
they wait for us to come home

Winter
by Lucas Hanson

Winter is filled with pleasant events.
Let me tell you what winter presents.
Fun games there are to play,
Even though the sky is grey.
So many things to do like sledding,
shoveling is something that I am dreading.
I look forward to building snowmen and forts.
But I do miss the days of wearing shorts!

Birthdays
by Jade Meuleners

Birthdays are exciting
But can also be frightening
You turn another age
And write a new page
It's your life's new chapter
While looking quite dapper
You love your savory cake
That your mother makes
You rip open your new gift
Then glide so swift
Sliding on your socks
While your sister mocks
And that's how birthdays go.

Words
by Olivia Desilets

I knead the words into my head as I am making bread.
Writing is like kneading bread, baking the words into my mind.
As it cooks I get more ideas for writing.
When the bread is done, I let it cool, and then I slice it, and I take a bite.
I taste words and I jot them down on paper.
The words become a poem.

My Favorite Shoes
by Colton Stark

When you can't find your shoes.
Those sneaky shoes, running away all the time
I never can find them ever.
It's like they fly away every day.
It's like magic.
Now I hate those shoes.

Rain
by Hayden Louk

Rain, it's a pain.
It comes in little drops.
It destroys things.
When it hits the ground it pops.
Rain, it's a pain.
May it pop and stop.
May it flop away,
like a flip flop.

Nature
by Quinlyn Brodeur

Nature is wild
So are we
God knows
Who we can be
Something inside us
Our future is like a book
Open chapters
Let's go look
Open doors
Help us see
No one can know
What glory we all seek

The Nights
by Mckenna Appelt

The sky turns off,
To let the stars shine bright
The wind blows softly,
To hear the grasses' quiet whistle
The snow stops falling
To let the flowers bloom bright
The bed covers unfold,
To let the children sleep under
The world keeps spinning,
To give the night and the day,
The soft snoring starts
To let the dreams begin
What happens in dreams,
No one knows for sure
They change all the time
But that's the fun
What we do know, though
Is the nights come and go,
To let the children wake up and shine

Summer Thoughts
by Margaret Flowers

In the summer the air is fresh and sweet,
and the water is clear and cools my feet.
The flowers are pink, they are red, they are blue,
they are yellow, they are white, they are violet too!
Will the flowers disappear, go away with fright,
or will they stay as the day turns to night.
The breeze may die down, making it hot,
but we children made lemonade, we made a lot!
We had fun in the water keeping us cool,
with squirt guns and water toys in the pool.
Will I sit inside tired out,
as the children play out and about?
For me will there be no more fun,
oh no, the summer has just begun!
The leaves on the trees dance in the sun,
as the breeze freely runs.
Oh the water is fresh and clear,
and yes the summer is finally here!

Summertime
by Colin Cox

Summertime is lots of fun
Swimming all day, ooh blazing hot sun
Playing outside almost every day,
See the ice cream truck, got to pay.
No school, we have a little break
Leaves haven't fallen yet, no need to rake
Summertime is lots of fun.
have two months off and I'm still not done
Going to places I've never been
The zoo, beach, how about a farm to see a hen
Summer is fun, so many different things
Ahh, I see a bee, hope it doesn't sting
Summer, summer my favorite season
As you can see here are all my reasons
Summertime is lots of fun
Playing with friends in the hot, blazing sun

Secrets, Secrets
by Brie Lawson

The wind whispers a secret,
It makes the trees dance,
Spreads joy to the hearts of the miserable,
It spreads happiness to the kind,
That unseen force is my companion,
It whistles through the cracks in the rocks,
When I'm running, it shrieks by my ears and tickles my face.
The sun warms my back with its unseen force,
When I lay on the sand, it smiles at me,
The sun's rays are then carried away on the back of the wind,
The water rushes past me,
It cannot whisper,
But it talks, and it gloats,
And it screams in my ears when it falls from a cliff,
When I run to the creek,
The wind whips my hair,
And the sun warms me,
And the water of the creek cools my feet,
This conversation between the water, wind, and the sun ... nature.

Elephant
by Abby Seeley

Elephant
Stomping cut
Running, walking, sleepy
Happy, loving, serious, mean
Elephant.

True Beauty
by Shannon Callaghan

When I was eight I took a trip
I took a trip somewhere that's beautiful
When I got there I was amazed
Amazed at how beautiful everything was
I loved it so much I didn't want to leave
I loved waking up to the sunrise
and going to bed with the sunset
I loved seeing the animals every day
I had the time of my life
What I saw in Africa changed my life
it changed my life because it was
True Beauty

Pencil
by Henley Mills

I got a pencil, so pretty and cute,
I used a stencil to draw a flute,
Then my cute pencil walked into the road,
I had to run with him to save him from getting too cold,
I gave it a hat,
It showed me some magic while I wrote about a bat,
The pencil just tells me what to talk about,
One time that pencil went swimming with me,
It made me feel happy and it was happy with me,
When it got too tiny for me to hold,
The pencil still smiled but had to be gone,
I smiled back in a shy way,
But it was time to throw him away,
Oh my poor pencil,
I want him back,
Take him out of that trash,
He's not too small,
Let him dance with me,
I know he can't write, but he still can read,
Let him run to me, please, please, please.

Winter Wonders
by Ginger Husband

There is a light above then sight
shining with a bright, bright light,
and with mythical creatures granting all wishes,
but when the summer wonders come out
the winter wonders go hide,
and the summers come out and stay for a while.

That Very Day
by Grace Luebke

That very day, was the day I became a Luebke.
That very day, I joined my forever family.
That very day, I became a little sister.
That very day, I finally belonged to someone.
That very day, I was no longer Riley.
That very day, I got a blessing from God.
That very day, I got my home sweet home.
That very day, God gave me to you, my new loving parents.
That very day, was the day I was adopted.
And that very day was October 4, 2005.

My First Ride
by Gracie Gomes

As the stable doors open
And the light starts to shine
We see a little pony
With bright blue eyes
As I saddled up
I was beginning to rise
Now that we have started
And trotted away
We went through the course
Without a second of delay
We leaped over the bars
And sped through the dust
We went so fast
That we did what we must
I am starting with a friend
That is more loyal than ever
She is also very clever
This is my poem
With love and care
If I don't win I will cry in despair

I Love You Because ...
by Liv Payne

I love you because
You are sincere, you listen when people need you most.
I love you because
You are loyal, you support me.
I love you because
You are trustworthy, I know you wouldn't lie to me.
I love you because
You are amiable, you treat us with empathy.
I love you because
You make me feel accepted.
You love me no matter what happens.
I love you because
You are exuberant, you personify joviality.
You are sincere, loyal, trustworthy, amiable,
accepting, exuberant, and affectionate.
You are my role model, hero, friend, teacher,
and always my advocate.

Me, the Sun and Moon
by Virginia Boggs

Daffodils are blooming, by the light of me
The summer wind blows and the grass sways, as if it's dancing.
As my light bears down onto the warmed beach sand.
When I look down at the gleaming ocean,
I see reflection of the dock,
Where fishermen are waiting for life to take the bait.
Another day has gone by, I have set again
Maybe now things will recognize me finally.
As the way I love.
And as the way I work.
And as the way I am.
Now as I turn into a different light.
I am the thing that provides light now, so Earth can see.
As I look down, I see a child,
She has lost everything, everything she loves, and even her own family.
She is lost in the big wide world.
She looks up and says,
"I do notice you oh sun and moon, I do appreciate your light.
I see the way you work at day, and the way you work at night."
Now that I know how it feels, there is nothing in the world
that will ever make me feel greater.

Music
by Zoë Lunzer

Music, its rhythms tasting bitter or sweet.
Also the tune, oh it's the tastiest treat.
Nothing is better than a soft melody
That can set anyone's soul free.
Now this voice can fly out, like it lives the words,
Flying with beauty, just like birds.
It's like the lyrics are a part of me
And will soar like angels, oh how it's so lovely.
Now plunking on the keys of the piano.
Songs, like trees, will start to grow.
These beauties made of love or hate
Leave me nothing to say other than music is great!

Dreamworks
by Eleanor Undem

From the moment my head hit the pillow, I slept with my stuffed armadillo.
My armadillo said to me, "Come on now, we're going deep sea!"
We went down under, the boats sounding like thunder,
And the fish paddled through the water. Next to me, slips through the sea, an otter.
We were seized by shadowed hands, dropped into no-man's land.
I stood at the gate, no way to escape.
Wrapped in isolation of my dreams, no sun nor moon gave light of beams.
For everything you hate, you became a piece of bait.
Your fears creep in around you, there is nothing you can do.
You're trapped without anywhere to run. You give up, your fears have you won.
This is a nightmare.
Just when you think you're dead, there is no more dread in your head.
You're pulled into the sky, my darling, you can fly!!
You soar up high on wings, you feel lifted on strings.
The treetops now your luscious floor,
You have no idea what your dreams have in store.
Your feet touch the ground, your head bears a crown.
You're queen of the town, you're sporting a lovely gown.
You're given a castle of gold, the keys to anything you now hold.
All the critters now your sidekick, your castle mounted next to a crick.
Like all great things, they come to an end, your wonderful things start to blend.
You start to wake up, you wish you could back up ...
Your dreams disappear, put back in your normal atmosphere.
Barely remembering your adventure, missing your nightly motion picture.

The Day I Played With My Friends
by Michelle Backhausen

One day I went to my friend's house and when we got there
we went on her deck and brought out some games.
The first game we played was Disney Uno and we each won a couple of rounds
Then after we played with Lego and I earned a really cool and large house
After we played something different, she said yes!
Then we played a cooking game.

The Amazing
by Sienna Regan

Reading, you are like a math problem that can never be solved
You can never be solved, because you are amazing
And amazing things cannot be solved
Amazing things could be solved but we as humans want the amazing things
To stay amazing
Because there are so many incredible things in this world
that need to stay amazing
And
Will stay amazing
- This poem was dedicated to my parents in which I love with all my heart
because they are amazing.

Luna
by Ava Wilmer

Such a beautiful sight,
Sometimes very slight.
Every week new shapes are amounted,
A deep slumber comes after the sheep were counted.
I have a face,
As the cow jumps it seems to chase.
Looking down with a little gaze,
But I will never be a vast blaze.
Some say I look kind of cheesy,
But that statement makes me feel uneasy.
I will always have many bright friends,
And they will be there until the very end.
Up in this tall black perch,
You don't even have to search.
For I am very old,
But bright as gold.
I have many dents,
And some of man's best accomplishments.
For I am the moon!

Summer To Fall
by Matthew Payes

Summer
Hot and sunny
You want to eat ice cream
School has ended
it starts to get cool
you want to wear pants
Summer is almost over
Summer is over
School starts
Fall

Fish
by Advitiya Srinivasan

Fish are loyal, fish are funny.
Everything's good, except when they're yummy.
Fish have fins, fish have scales.
Fish can be female, fish can be male.
They can be blowfish, they can be stonefish.
They can be minnows, they can be goldfish.
Fish can be crazy, fish can be lazy.
It's nice to be in the world of fish,
For a year or maybe 2 ...
Well I wish!

The Mud Cycle
by Lauren Woody

Do you ever think about mud?
I think most people don't.
Just imagine the life of mud
They get stomped and never get noticed
Only by little children
Who like to make mud pies.
But just when the mud is really happy
The children grow up and say goodbye
They move away, leaving the mud
alone, sad, and heartbroken
It sits there untouched for a couple of years
Wishing someone would come to play
Then a new family moves in
And the little children play with the mud.
Once again the mud is happy
It's the mud cycle!

Ode To Steak
by Sophie Jones

A hunk of goodness
Big and thick
Always the best
Not long to pick
It smells so good
That my mouth waters
It's nice and warm
And nice to his daughters
In my mouth
It's having a party
A meat party in fact
And no one's tardy
Oh, juicy steak
I love it so much
It's good and juicy
And has a magical touch

What's Under My Bed
by Marybeth Hallberg

My American Girl doll,
A couple posters I got at the mall,
A piece of gum I found in a hall,
An old phone that can't even make a call,
A piece of my Christmas part that said "and peace to all."
My stuffed animal cat,
My blue stocking hat,
My old baseball bat,
My sister's welcome mat,
My fake, plastic rat
Shh! My pet monkey, Tickles,
My outdated jar of pickles,
A couple dimes and a lot of nickels,
A portable freezer with my icicles
My wooden painting easel,
A map of Brazil,
A puddle of a Kool-Aid spill,
A really big shirt from Goodwill,
Probably a ten dollar bill
What's under my bed?

If I Was an Eagle
by Margot Peterson

If I was an eagle
I would fly around all day
I would perch in treetops
and look for prey.
I would eat fish for dinner
I would eat worms for lunch
I would rest in my nest
of leaves, sticks and mud

The Evil Homework Monster
by Meghan Hembree

Johnny was bored and throwing a fit,
math problems being torn up in his midst.
He broke his pencil, screamed and yelled,
until finally he said, "I want to eat a little."
Johnny ran downstairs, cheeks blotched red,
and what he saw made him sure he'd bonked his head.
A monster, dripping with dread, looked Johnny in the eye.
He would have fled, but the monster kindly said,
"Only three hundred pages to go ... "
The monster was made of homework papers,
impossible questions, his mouth made of a red stapler.
Claws formed from tricky questions,
and to avoid death, Johnny yelled, "I HATE MATH PROBLEMS!"
The monster swelled and said with anger,
"Homework isn't a danger. Problems are noble,
and you can very well solve them!
You are doing very well at these tricky math problems."
And poor Johnny stood in the room as the monster cast its spell of doom,
A light went into the young boy,
who was prodded by the monster like he was a toy.
"Homework lovers, hear my words! All the haters of me will soon turn!
For I am the Homework Monster, and one more is under my spell!"
The monster left with one last hiss, and Johnny's twisted brain thought this:
"Homework is noble, a great work of art!
It is now the greatest joy in my heart!"
His light-filled eyes kept glowing, now not sure of what he was knowing.
He finished his torn homework, much to surprise,
and ran through the streets, crying out to the world,
"Homework Monster, I am forever yours!"
Johnny wasn't the last to fall under the spell.
Someday, maybe you will as well ...

Sports
by Mason Kinnahan

Basketball
uniforms, hoops
passing, dribbling, blocking
dunks, jams, assists, stealing
running, catching, passing
players, coaches
Football

Flowers
by Victoria Quirk

Flowers, we are a beautiful thing.
But we are only here in the summer or spring.
I look up and watch the birds fly by
and see little raindrops falling from the sky.
There are many of us. Tulips, roses, daisies and more.
We treat each other equally like never before.
When the days get colder, I know it's time to go.
I look at my petals hanging real low.
It's a real bummer.
But I can't wait to see you all next summer.

My Name
by Savanna Anchell

You thought that I left you as you screamed my name
as you say where is she, where is she
the doctors crowded around you, now you cannot see my face
wondering did she leave, she left without saying goodbye
now screaming my name again, the pain in your voice struck my heart
I said I'm here, I didn't leave you, I'm right here
but little did I know this would be the last you say my name

She ...
by Talya Moorman

Her skin is the color of rich wheat on a field,
Her eyes are the color of a springtime blue sky,
Her hair the color of the thousands of grains of sand on a beach,
She is curious and brave, but agile.
She glows like a shooting star in the nighttime sky,
she is beautiful, not only by her looks and style,
but her friendliness and her kind heart,
now I know 'tis she, she is the one to marry.

Nature
by Carter Wilson

Mountain
Cold, Snow
Climbing, Sleeping, Hunting
Rock, Goat, Shark, Fish
Swimming, Exploring, Fishing
Warm, Water
Ocean

Family
by Alexa Toenyan

Family
Happy, joyful
Loving, caring, sharing
Families do a lot together
Relative

Excitement
by Thomas Holmquist

Excitement is when football season comes around
And all my energy is already found.
The excitement builds while I put on my gear
And I am feeling no fear.
On my jersey it has my number, it has my name
The crowd cheers as I play the game.
With the energy that abounds
I tackle my opponents to the ground.
My excitement continues as I run down the field
I catch a pass, that's a big deal!
The cheering continues as I move down the field
I love the excitement that I feel.

The Poem About Poems
by Hayden Miller

This is a poem about poems.
Poems can be different but still the same.
Some poems rhyme and others don't (this poem doesn't).
A poem could be about something, like for example, poems.
Some poems are important, others not so important.
Poems could be funny, or sad, or just made for the fun of it.
While poems are all different, they could have the same meaning,
but this poem is unlike any other, mostly because it is about poems

Summertime
by Samantha Bobeck

Summertime means watching the sunset every day,
Watching the dogs play fetch.
Watching the squirrels jump from tree to tree.
Summertime, it's when my family goes to Colorado,
When we arrive, we go to a Ren Fair, after we set up,
We also celebrate my birthday.
Summertime brings happy smiles,
Summertime brings swimming pools out.
Summertime brings bikes out,
Summertime is the best time of year,
Summertime brings families closer.

Trusting
by Alice Smith

There are people in our lives that we can't trust
But sometimes we must.
Trust is a gust,
Of power.
It's sometimes a flower,
But others,
Shameful towers.
Oh, please give an hour!
I will be trust full,
So you can pull out,
That trust that you knew I had.

The Poem
by Nick D'Amato

"Hey! We are in a poem!"
he yelled obnoxiously
"Should we rhyme?"
He replied
"How can we live like this?
There's no food or water?
Only words on paper!"
"The words don't even come from our mouths!"
"We don't have mouths!"
"Over all!"
He started then simultaneously recited:
"This is boring!"

May
by Ava Rousseau

The air is warm
The flowers are blooming
The grass is green
The birds are singing
Trees grow big and tall
School is almost out
Everyone is happy
The children scream and shout
The sun sets bright and pretty
Summer is drawing near
The birds leave their nest
This means May is here.

Soccer
by Nataly Mejia Climaco

I love soccer.
Soccer is the best sport in the whole world.
Soccer is the center of the universe.
Soccer is to die for.
Soccer is joyful and hopeful,
But, the best thing about soccer is,
That you can have fun and shoot some goals.
Goooaaalll!
Even if you don't win,
You still get to have fun with your friends playing soccer!

My Bearded Dragon
by Kaylee Briggs

Spiky, sharp
As feisty as can be,
And, looks so amazing.
She is as fast as lightning,
She is love in my heart,
She runs like the wind
And sends
A look of love in her eyes,
Flying past me like a plane.
She is kind and giving in her heart,
I love her so much,
That I hope my heart melts before hers.

Friends vs. Enemies
by Jack Abrahamson

Friends
Nice, kind
Caring, laughing, helping
God, cash, strangers, Devil
Unrewarding, stealing, bullying
Mean, alone,
Enemies

Feelings
by Abby Zitzmann

Mad
Unhappy, frown
Stomping, not welcoming, not respecting
Red face; not red face
Welcoming, respecting, loving
Smile, nice
Happy

Waterfalls
by Jadelyn Taylor

Rushing white water
Water tumbling from above
Glinting in the sun
Waterfalls come down in a flash
And you can hear a noise splash
Whinstone and shale rapidly collapse
The power is fantastic
The waterfall loud
And the beauty of this sight standing above the clouds

Dreams ...
by Maggie McCabe

Why do we have dreams that make us bet?
Why do we have dreams that make us regret?
Dreams can be amazing, wonderful, fun!
Dreams can be scary and make us run!
They can be funny, silly and make us all happy.
They can be weird, crazy and make us all sappy.
But dreams can be outgoing and wild,
Which helps me to be a fun, loving child!

Pets
by Cooper Pesek

Cats
Calm, Sleepy
Jumping, Climbing, Meowing
Always snuggly, Always playful
Running, Barking, Digging
Playful, Hungry
Dogs

Spring
by Alex Nephew

Spring, spring
has finally sprung
it will soon be summer fun,
I hope it will never be done
because I am having so much fun
In spring

The Sun
by Lizeth Sanchez

The sun is always smiling
She peeks through the trees
She is a star
She has a bright personality
She is hot and humongous,
But she still is sweet.
She guides me through day,
And she is a baby chick ...
She always brightens my day.

The Music Showdown
by Frankie Dusenka

Music flowing through the air,
Try to outplay me if you dare.
I practice like a calendar, day after day.
Ooh, a talent show you say?
Zoom to town is what I'll do,
And I'll do it to beat you.
You played music better there.
You outplayed me fair and square.

Liberty We Say, Liberty We Get!
by Josue Blanco

From the fight with Great Britain
To the Constitution which was written.
America has been strong
For more than 200 years long.
We were ruled by a king
Which was really a horrendous thing.
We are finally free
Freedom, independence, and liberty!

Weekends
by Clarence D Johnson IV

On the weekends I watch TV
On the weekends I play
On the weekends I play basketball
On the weekends I play soccer ball
On the weekends I play with dog
On the weekends I go to the beach
On the weekends I go to sleep
On the weekends sometimes I dab
On the weekends I play Minecraft
On the weekends it's like with a panda
On the weekends it's like you're drinking Fanta
When I sleep I hear "snore, snore"
When I play I hear "peep, peep"

Cheeseballs
by Michelle Murphy

Cheeseballs are great!
Cheeseballs are like little clouds covered with ... cheese!
Cheeseballs like to go on roller coasters,
they especially like "escape the giant rocks, and into the abdomen pool!"
Cheeseballs may look like adorable little unicorns, except ...
at 12:31 at night they rise, from, from,
from the cheeseball container. Dun! Dun! Dun!
They roll out of the container one by one never leaving a "man" behind,
well uh ... let's just leave that idea behind (*awkward silence*).
Anyways, they roast marshmallows on the stovetop near Mom's teakettle!
They talk about their plan, but ... the clock strikes 6:59 AM!
The time when ... the family wakes up! Dun! Dun! Dun!
They quickly hop into the container, the big purple disk gently flying
on top of the container, every cheeseball covered in bacteria.

Candy
by Landyn Remer

Very sadly, Sandy took my candy
I thought it was madly
it made me madder than a fire ant on fire
melting the water
going through a volcano
mad as can be
but I got more
candy

Leaves
by Natalie Lacko

The red ones are as red as cardinals
The yellow ones are as yellow as the sun
The orange ones are like a sunset going down
And the bearing cold will never change
until the amazing summer will take ...

Boredom
by Klara Kett

Boredom fills my mind with irritation,
while I try to think of what I knew.
I don't have any motivation,
and not the slightest idea of what to do.
My mind is emptier than a poor man's wallet,
and when I open the doors to the closet,
I find nothing new.
I didn't think it could be so annoying,
when the difficulty of searching grew.
Running through my mind I search,
trying to find a clue.
But all there is in my mind is a smirch,
preventing me from looking through.
I sit and ponder of what I could do,
but then I realize I'm not in the mood.
I decide to pet my cat until he starts to purr,
but once he walks away, my mind is again a blur.
I go outside to watch the birds,
but they're nowhere to be found.
So, instead, I take a walk in the forest, and pick out every small sound,
and everything I see, I watch, until they leave, and continue my stroll.

The Man
by Sean Sargent

There once was a man who was tall
Although his son was very small
But his dog was big
But he could not dig
The dog's favorite season was fall

Nibble, the Class Hamster
by Ngoc Tran

When I saw him, I squealed like a pig!
He crawled into my heart,
He is fast as lightning,
And mighty as can be.
He is sweet as pie,
And smooth as soft fabric,
But fierce as a lion!

The Beach
by Nick Young

The heat, baking me in the solar rays.
We got a kite at the beach cafe.
My feet swelling in the blazing sand!
Sure hope they get tanned.
The waves splashing in the cool blue water.
Playing football with my father.
The beach isn't far away,
Looking at the water from a stairway.

The Wandering Mind
by Gracie Skalsky

I think of pink,
Also a mink,
Pink mink I think,
I think of a chip,
That had a big lip,
And ate a ship,
The ship got mad,
And then very sad,
It read an ad,
That was very bad,
And went to its granddad,
Who was very rad.

Bob, Keven, and Fill
by Aidan Poe

Bob is red, Keven is blue, Bob is a blob, Keven is 7,
But don't forget their cousin, Phill who is a pill,
who's chilling on the beach, acting like a bill.

Silent Night
by Ashlyn Stone

Silent night
No light
The moon peaks
The mouse squeaks
Then everything is still
Silent sky
The bird will fly
But not until morning
Dawn breaks
Everyone wakes
I run with all my might
Silent night

Manifest Deatheny: An Indian's Perspective
by Kaya Graham

I maybe like all the sights I see,
but I do not like the Manifest Destiny
For I maybe die of starvation or disease,
but I will always still love my family,
for one has died, my heart stops pumping,
do I deserve to live with life jumping?
Now we have food 'cause of John Ross,
so now we don't feel so lost.

The Business Flying Sea Animal
by John Krupa

"You owe this crab six thousand clams,"
said Sir Eh the business flying sea animal.
"I don't owe nothing,"
said Bob the eel.
"Don't lie to me or I'll squirt you with my ...
dramatic pause ... water gun."
"Okay, okay I do owe him six thousand clams."
Then Bob paid the crab.
And Eh still squirted him with his water gun.

The Dark Night
by Mirari Paredes-Tinoco

You hear the dark night sound
and you fall down and down.
You feel the soft white pillow
and with the sheets will make you mellow.
You dream and dream.
Into a deep night sleep.
You open your eyes and you see something bright
and you know it's not the arctic cold night ...

Motorbikes
by Sean Raboin

As the bikes line up to start their engines waiting to depart
"Hear the Go!" The crowd screaming "Give us a show!"
Waving the bikes, the flag is like a horse whip in the air
The bikes depart, jumping holes and dodging poles
Before you know it the bikes cross the finish. I won
When I won my hands were in the air like I just do not care!

The Fit
by Krish Jain

My friend was throwing a fit
So I told him to sit
But he started yelling and his tongue got bit
And then it was me he started to hit
But then he decided to go over to Mit
And then my friend fell in a pit
Me and Mit thought it was lit
But then Mit started throwing a fit about his zit
I think my friend's anger really did emit

Walt Disney World
by Gracie Gabbert

Off to the castle to see the firework show
It'll be so beautiful I can't wait to go
The rides are a thrill
I hope I don't scream but I probably will
Ariel, Goofy, and Mickey too
Maybe I'll find Cinderella's shoe
The day at Disney is always the best
I'll have to go home and rest

A Champion
by Zakkary Ober

A receiver named Edelman
Was a very nice gentleman
He had a big beard
That everyone feared
Now a Super Bowl champion

Roses
by Jade Melvin

Roses are pretty
Roses are sweet
Roses may be a butterfly's treat
Roses may poke, maybe they'll scratch
Roses will always grow in a patch

Puppy Love
by Jenna Carlson

Floppy ears
Funny faces
Wants to play
While you tie your laces
Running, jumping,
Playing around
While you're playing
On the ground
Floppy ears
Funny faces
Puppy love
Lick the faces

My Friend
by McKenzie Guardia

Kind and awesome
She is my friend
In my family, of course
Caring and pretty
She is like the sun shining on me!
She is sweet as candy and really handy!
Pretty as a flower
but she is not a coward
Oh, how I love her so
my dear mom

The Monkey
by Abbi Paquette

There once was a chunky monkey
The monkey was just so funky
They love bananas
Also love nanas
And now all he acts is punky

The Bear Who Didn't Care
by Mialyn Dunn

The bear was at the fair
as he stared at his hair
they thought he was funny
until they saw a bunny
and then the bear had no care

Blue
by Muhammad Mazwan

Blue is the animated color of rain
Or what Mr. McGrew used to write in the board
Persuade, inform and entertain
If you don't like blue then that's a shame
Blue is the color of Sam's jacket
And I think that it's lit (Well a bit)
Blue is the color of the rain, and it's sad
Which is 100% really bad
Blue is the color of Sam's shoe, and he has two
Sometimes I go, "Koo koo!!!"
Blue likes you, so be in a good MOOD
Roses are red, violets are blue
That is actually 100 percent true
Blue is the color of your cry,
some people do it because they're shy
Blue is the color of the sky, every child keeps asking why
Cool kids would go crazy, especially Hemze
Blue is the color of the sea
The color of water
I miss Jason Lee
I can't stop thinking
about Sam's shoe
All of these examples are for
BLUE

Alex
by Nick Stueven

Alex is tall
And likes to play football
He likes to punt
And hunt
He is my friend
To the end
He is smart
And has a big heart

Summer
by Robert Krause

Summer
hot, sunny
swimming, running, hiking
going on a vacation
biking, climbing, camping
warm, rainy
Spring

The Bee of Poetry
by Ella Tennant

Poetry is life
Poetry is my feelings
It's like a bee buzzing
A bee making me see my purpose
The true things inside of me
I'm letting it all out on this piece of paper
All of the true me
The things they cannot see
The bee it buzzes, it makes me see my purpose
And my purpose is poetry
Poetry helps me let out all I've been holding in
When the light goes dark and they cannot see
It comes out, everything inside of me
The love, the fear, the excitement
Everything ends up here
On this piece of paper
Poetry makes me free
Poetry is the true me
Thanks to the bee,
The buzzing bee inside of me

The Blue Ghost
by Hunter Erlick

There once was a ghost that was blue
That was almost as ugly as you
That's a challenging thing to do
We were talking about your life too

My Mom
by Delaney Clements

My mom likes cupcakes
She likes confetti cakes
She has a lot of money
She makes smoothies with honey
She loves to bake

Thoughts
by Ariana Henriquez

Some people ignore them
Some people hear them
And trust them
Some people live by them
They give you ideas
They give you nightmares
They pick you up
They bring you down
But at the end
They're just ...
Thoughts

This Is Me
by Riplee Saurer

Riplee
Is a sister, a daughter, and a friend
Loves my families, God, and my friends
Is good at gymnastics, school, and being a friend
Feels happy, loved, excited
Needs my siblings, my sleep, and fresh air
Wants my pets, my sleep, and to be a teacher
Fears spiders, hurting someone, and scary movies
Likes to eat strawberries, candy, chocolate
Watches brother, sisters, and niece and nephew
Is a resident of Minnesota
Saurer

California
by Madeline Knoell

Over the sun-kissed hills and plains of California
the sweet song of the birds sing as they flap their tropical wings.
In the long days we play, kicking luscious green grass under our toes.
Surfing's such a blast, only the waves know where we may go.
And we love art, we have painters and sculptors and drawers galore.
Some of us are wacky but geniuses aren't sane.
This life I would trade for no other thing because my heart belongs in California.

Soccer
by Hemze Kurban

It was such a good sport,
Like me going to Dulles Airport,
It was gazing,
It was soccer,
The goalkeeper a.k.a. blocker,
My friend said he stalks me playing soccer,
So guess what, I called him a stalker.

Real Friends
by Rizelle Cayabyab

Don't ever forget your friends at all
Real friends pick you up when you fall
They pick you up so you can just stand tall
Don't ever think your friendship is just a take and hold
But friendship costs more than gold

Love
by Josephine Stevens

Love feels like a cool wind on your face,
or warm sun on your back,
love is the gold sand,
outlining the turquoise sea of positive energy,
love drives you toward your goals,
your dreams,
your determination,
your best self,
accept the love,
the sand, the ocean,
the dreams, the goals,
the determination,
your best self.

St. Patrick's Day
by Margo Beyer

My father's name is Pat,
I'm quite fond of that.
He's not 6 inches tall,
And he doesn't fall.
He doesn't own any gold,
But he sure is bold.
Taking care of us kids,
Me and my sis.

Spring
by Eric Kugel

In spring, all the flowers will bloom,
the snow will melt, and with it the gloom.
Mowing the lawn for the first time that year,
out into the grass romp out the deer.
The sun comes out and shines bright,
it gives the world all of its light.
All the children go out to play,
especially if it is a nice day.
April showers bring May flowers,
only stay in if you are a coward!
Go to the beach, play in the sand,
listen to the waterside band.

Christmas Eve
by Grace Lavan

I wake to the sound of the warm happy fire,
Its heat and light I do admire,
along with its marvelous sound.
Yet what is better than the diamond-like snow,
just the sight of it makes my heart glow.
The clock sounds midnight but I haveth no sleep
I creep down the stairs making not a peep.
I race to the kitchen, tear open the cupboard,
grabbing a mug reading, "Merry Christmas, My Brother!"
I fill it with cocoa and marshmallows with cheer,
and prance around like a small reindeer.
I drink it up quick and scurry in to bed,
as dreams of paradise sneak into my head.
Merry Christmas to me,
Merry Christmas to you,
Merry Christmas to all who believe.

A Tree's Love
by Melanie Caro

Trees, trees, you have beautiful leaves, and gorgeous bark.
Your sap smells wonderful, and your acorns make great decorations.
Your wood is useful.
You make homes for animals, and a quiet place to read.
You are the best listener, and my best friend.

On the Racetrack
by Isabel D'mello

All you see is a blur
All you hear are hooves hitting the ground
You know death is in your shadow
One wrong move and that's it
You're moving at blinding speed
You can make out a shape in front
You see the finish wire
You squeeze your knees together
You win
You pull back on the reins
You slow down
The crowd cheers
You survived

Willow Tree and I
by Hannah Bang

I looked up at a willow tree
Gone through so much, just like me
I have gone through pain and sorrow
Eating me up with a pain in my heart
This tree has gone through storms and blizzards
Fire ripping through forests, ashes aflame
I have gone through joy and peace
A soothing touch like petals on a soft breeze
This tree has seen spring, with light dew on its tip
The chirp of new birds, the wind soothing its tired heart
I have gone season through season
Watching my soul grow old and wise
This tree has been bitten by the wolves of winter,
The life of spring, the heat of summer, the flutter of fall
This tree and I, we've gone through so much
We've seen our kin die, been blown by the wind of life
And it's now our time to finally rest, this willow tree and I

Snowflakes
by Eva Murray

White flakes in the sky
Very happily fly by me
So very beautiful.

The Hot Summer Days
by Samantha Petron

I love to go to the cooling pool and play,
I do it all the time, all day!
I also like to go to the hot playground,
and every time, I bring my furry pet hound!

My Friend
by Chasey Fleck

I know this cat whose name is Sue,
She has this friend whose name is Boo,
He scares her a lot,
But then he gets caught,
Now he wants to write his haiku

Birds
by Eric Detjen

Birds are turds, their friends are nerds
There are herds of birds split in thirds
some are furred some are stirred
and some are antbirds

Me
by Kelby Pierson

Is brother, son, sibling
Loves God, Jesus, family
Is good at hockey, football, baseball
Feels good, happy, sad
Needs food, God, a family
Wants to see God, to see Jesus, to go to Heaven
Fears dark, dying, being alone in the dark
Likes to eat tacos, pizza, super cheesy nachos
Watches TV, YouTube, videos
Is a resident of Minnesota

Oh, Trinidad and Tobago
by Aaron Bhowansingh

It is very hot,
Beautiful sights everywhere,
Family members.

Trees
by Drew Austin

Branches dancing
Cracking, crashing, falling trees
Strong wind wins the day.

Cent
by Evelyn Barnett

A cent went flying into a vent,
And in that vent was a tent,
That spent its last cent,
On a Portland cement rent tent.

Do You?
by Caleb Underwood

Do you like one or two.
Do you like to make goo?
Do you like to rhyme?
Would you like to watch a mime?
Do you like to get new stuff?
Would you like to write a haiku?
Do you have a dime?
It is time for me to go

Happy Birthday, Dr. Seuss!
by Ella Ronci

Dear Dr. Seuss,
Thank you for writing good books about moose
(And lots of other things!)
I just want you to know what happiness it brings.
My family enjoys them both day and night,
In the dark and in the light.
So, "Happy Birthday, Dr. Seuss!"
(Your birthday is on March 'tooth!') (March second)

Moon Reflects
by Nadia Pevestorf

The moon reflects across the ocean
it sleeps in the up
all the stars get up at the same time.
It comes up in the night
it shimmers and it shines
all through the night.
Stars shimmer and shine
and the moon sparkles on the ocean.

Sunset
by Chiara Ciavarri

Sun setting low,
Sinking into the lake,
A yellow lemon,
That tastes not sour,
But sweet.
The lake smiles and dances,
As the sun falls into it.
The colors dance and sing their blessing,
To the sun.
Red for bless,
Blue for you,
Pink and purple mixed for children.
The stars.

A Dream
by Natalie Hall

I have a dream about world peace,
That one day all the fighting will cease.
The world will no longer be grim.
The world won't be as dim.
That maybe happiness will start to stir.
No more sadness will occur.
There will be hope and love,
It will be because of our Father from above.
Until then we can only think,
About what will make this country link.
Let's thank the Lord for all He's done,
But the journey has only just begun.

Hidden Beauty
by Valeria Dancea

Beaver is building his home
Hawk is hunting, watching like a garden gnome
Frog is croaking peacefully
Chipmunk sitting in a tree
Dragonfly is buzzing by
Birds sing songs as they fly
Snake is staring, looking at me
All in the swamp
The place of hidden beauty

Where the Sand Meets the Sea
by Michaelah Hancock

I come to the beach, the soft sand underneath me
and the water right above me.
Rolling waves chase me
but I always escape them,
because they make me do what I love.
The sun shining so bright
that all I can see is light.
I see the coral down below
but see the people up high.
I sit down on the towel and think
what is the best time to come back?
Hey! I've got it, never leave.

Tears
by Jacob Johnson

Why do all good things slip away
Why can't these good things just stay
We don't want to say okay
But all good things must slip away
For in the deepest darkest times, one light still shines
Those who enter the light will be saved, even if they've misbehaved
But all good things we never before craved must slip away
And at the end of twilight we will always know what's right,
for good things must slip away, when they have no more reasons to stay
So in this way we must say goodbye today before it slips away
For it takes tears tomorrow to bring a memory from today
And for the last time I say, all good things must slip away
- In Remembrance of Scott Nocton

The Cardinal
by Ella Montanus

Winter has come with no color in sight.
Clouds pure gray, snow pure white.
Sure, winter can be fun
Even though there is no sun
But I long for spring every night
Blank, boring days make me depressed
I want colorful birds, singing their best.
But I saw a bird that stayed
Which surprised me that day
But it also made me impressed.
That little bird did not care about the snow
Its ruby red wings stretched out were a show
A bright color in winter I found kind of rare
It was just one color that brought me out of despair
And helped me ignore that bitter wind blow.
But that little red cardinal could not stay
And has to leave this very day.
It was great to see some color rise
Catching the attention of my eyes
Before it flew away.

Garden of Secrets
by Graceanna Stecyk

Deep underground where secrets are fool,
Flowers are ocean blue surrounding water. a starry pool,
They've heard wishes and dreams so quiet and serene,
Whispering quotes so quiet and unseen,
They've seen wars and deaths,
They are past, present and future alike,
If only memories could fly they would've been gone a long time ago,
They've heard secrets and lies and repeat the sayings each time,
They have no beginning or end, never ever dead,
A garden of secrets unheard and untold
covered in scars, they are getting old,
One day 5 are gone, then 4, then 3, then 2, until only 1 was left,
A girl, a child, found the blossom and said words from the surface,
The sun, the waters, everything had a purpose,
The last flower withered and died, the garden of secrets is gone,
The broken dreams and withered wishes,
Gone,
People grieve and cry,
But do not know that memories never disappear and the seeds of the past,
present and future still are dormant serene, unseen,
They just need more secrets, wishes, dreams to grow.

My Family
by Tamar Chodos

Welcome to our happy home
Peek in, what do you see?
Let us introduce ourselves
We're the Chodos family.
Osnat's twenty-one and she's the biggest,
Of the kids in the Chodos crew.
Yoni and Nadav are the best biggest brothers,
I think they know you too.
Next comes a sister, her name is Tamar,
She's quiet and she's fun.
Then comes her seven year old brother,
His name is Noam.
Our family is just like yours,
As our daily stories will show.
We'll work hard, make choices,
And from our mistakes we'll grow!
So come and join us on the couch,
Where we'll ask, think, and discuss.
We'll learn things about ourselves,
It will be like a trip for us!

Gemstones
by James Foss

There's thulite and smithsonite and all that quartz,
There's sugilite and topaz and some stones cure warts.
Bloodstone and tourmaline and all kinds of rubies,
Rhyolite and emerald which can cure diabetes.
Kyanite and garnet and all kinds of pearls,
Jasper and rose quartz are adored by girls.
Some stones like peacock ore conduct electricity,
And Seattle is known as the emerald city.
From amethyst to labradorite to gold is a range,
Combined stones can look really strange.
Coral is a gemstone too,
So are some minerals (I thought they told you).
Fluorite has a lot of color,
Give a gemstone for a present to your mother.
Apophyllite and galena and chlorite galore,
Chalcedony and cerussite and lots more.
I will end there so don't be sad,
But let me just say: gemstones are rad!

A Book
by Rosemarie Jones

The cover is a wall
protecting all within
knowledge
on pages
telling a tale
of splendor
sadness
romance
or just a life
all within those walls

I Want To Be Alone
by Anzal Bashir

when you want to be alone
you've got the blues
you want to sit in a dark room.
you toss and turn
but you don't know what to do.
But yet you don't want to talk
about what you've been through.
So you just sit in that dark room.

Happy Birthday
by Chaya Dalya Berezovsky

I love my birthday because it makes me feel so happy.
it is special because you turn another age.
I pick something to do and it is always so much fun.
last year when I went to Crayola Experience,
I heard kids laughing and having fun.
At home, I smell the yummy cake in the oven.
I am so excited to see what it looks like and tastes like.
I love when we take pictures with my family, balloons and cake.
I feel so happy when we do that.
I taste the birthday cake and it is so delicious.
The flavor of the cake is so awesome and the frosting is too.
The ice cream feels so cold on my throat and in my mouth.
It is so yummy and super great.
I am so excited for my birthday.
I know it will be so much fun in New York this year.

Mom
by Maryjane Vazquez-Silva

Mom, you are the best mom ever.
Whenever I say "Can you help me"
You say "Yes."
When I'm sad you make sure I'm happy.
Whenever I fall you help me get up.
When I'm tired you say "go to sleep, you don't want to get up late."
When I'm bored you say "where you wanna go?"
I say "anywhere."
Mom, you're the best mom ever.

Ecuador
by Giseld Mera Morocho

Ecuador, a little lovely country with beautiful great views
from far distance or close by views
and every person in it love to dance and sing
from people living free in the mountains
to people living in big cities.
Every person visit each other even if they are far away or close to each other.
They all love each other, animals to humans, humans to animals.
And every party they laughed and dance
and always remember where they are, stepping on Ecuador.

The Quiet Place
by Makenzie Lambert

This place is very quiet. I love the quiet so I can read,
if someone disturbs the quiet they will be hushed
then it will be silent again.
The books on each shelf are so overwhelming
I can never choose!
When I finally choose a book,
I go sit down and read.
I look up from my book and look around
I see others quietly reading
And some people searching on the computers.
I smile and start reading again.
Suddenly I'm tapped on the shoulder
Now it is time to go!
I check out my book and then we leave.
I hope we can come back to the library again soon!

Red
by Saoirse Donegan

Red is warmth;
Like a hot summer day;
As warm as a campfire on a cold December day.
Red.

Spring
by Abby Stewart

The wind sang all day,
Tall bright grass is dancing in the wind.
Butterflies are doing cool tricks in the park.
Moss is overlapping the gray rock.
Rain is flying in the city.
The sun sleeps at night.

Pencil
by Yurem Alejandro-Reyes

A pencil is a long yellow stick with an eraser and a pointy end.
The pencil calls my name to use it.
I use the pencil for homework, to draw.
I use it for many things like for spring on my fingers
and tricks and catching it by the end of the eraser.
That's how I have fun.

This Land
by Riya Patil

We saw this land
Oh, beauty it was
We were relieved for not traveling anymore
People became better from the horrible diseases
We landed on this land to have freedom
To practice our own religion
To do what we wanted
To not to be controlled by the rulers
We love this land
Not just for the rich stuff
But for the opportunities we have
To sharing this land with other people
We now know this land
It is now part of our life
We have known it for 400 years
We will never ever leave it

Advice/Hice
by William Freeman

Hey there all you gentlemen.
I'm Mr. Ben, but call me Ken.
When you are sick just chew a stick.
That's my advice but I call it hice.
Bye, make sure to wear a tie.

Boring
by Davion Wallace

Sitting staring
You sit for a minute and you sit
For an hour or you lay down and do nothing.
You can see how it feels lazy
and my mind is not thinking of nothing
and my hands fell asleep and my feet fell asleep

My Loving Brother
by Katie Cardwell

My loving, loving brother
I know you get frustrated at me
But I know you still love me unconditionally
I know I bug you sometimes
But I just want to play
You always yell at me
but I will love you forever and ever
even if I yell at you I want you to know ...
I will love you unconditionally
- Dedicated to my brother Cody

Mall of America
by Brenda Jaimes Morales

Many games to play
Many stores to go
and many stairs to climb
Many clothes to buy
and many games to ride
guess how many Nick characters I saw
I saw Spongebob, Ninja Turtles
and many other characters, so many to hug.
By and by so many people to see
by the end of time they're all gone.

Moonlight
by Sam Wawersik

Horses gallop across the metallic beach.
The moon shines down on a horse's silver mane.
The rain comes crashing down like little stars alighting from the heavens.

Wolves
by Renay Simon

Howling wolves are trotting.
Through the beautiful sunny.
Alaskan tundra.

Colors
by Alana Reese

Colors
Fade, glaze, glow
Brightness, glimmer, dye, tint
Highlight, overlap, sparkle
Glowing, hot
Neon

The Pencil Comic
by Armand Bajula

The pencil snapped and screamed
"Ouch!"
The pencil whined on and on for glue
What did pencil do?
He got some glue!
The end.

The Beach
by Sophia Arnold

Seagulls flying through the skies,
Fish riding with the tides,
Turtles moseying around,
Hermit crabs digging in the ground,
Starfish lying in the sun,
Giant crabs on the run,
Dolphins jumping with amazing heights,
The beach has such wonderful sights

Summer
by Anna Fiddelke

Splashing in the waves
Spreading out the big blanket
Toes in the sand. Play.

Dreams
by Ariana Quinteros

Dreams
Inspire, imaginative
Sleeping, encouraging, confusing
We dream to achieve
Uplifting, changing, concerning
Sweet, loving
Vision

School
by Margot Jauert

School is for talking and walking
Playing and laying
Turning and learning
Trying but not lying
School is for fun so ...
We are never done

Spring
by Hailey Ly

Springtime
When the snow melts
When flowers start to sprout
Bears come out of hibernation
Seedling

Summer Days, August Ways
by Laney Hillman

The summer flies by
the sun goes fast
as the birds chirp
and the flowers grow vast
As the sun goes down
and the children go to sleep
There's no sound except a gentle creak

Bunnies
by Rachel Fritton

Bunnies are so cute and fuzzy,
They will never be more cuddly.
If they were up in the sky,
They would need some wings to fly.
Bunnies are the cutest thing,
They should not be used to fling.
Bunnies have the cutest eyes,
You cannot tell them lies.

The Life of Spring
by Isaiah Fafard

The flowers are blooming like
the sun coming over the horizon
The wind is blowing across fields like a hurricane
The grass is turning green
The sky is blue like the sea
And everything is coming to life

The Lion Outside My Door
by Ben Refsell

The lion outside my door
though I never hear him roar
I know he is there
but I just can't bear
to share my room with him
not because he will bite or fight
but because it would be quite tight
me in one room with a lion

4th of July
by Gunnar Jacobson

Parties everywhere, grills cooking
I can smell sweet watermelon, juicy burgers and corn on the cob
Fireworks amidst me light up the sky at thousands of ball games
Almost as if millions are being set off at once
Hot July summer days
Sweating and exhausted from playing
Time to jump into the pool!
As the night ends we go see firework shows
Amazing day.

Summer
by Mark Beranek

When daisies are out and you're not being lazy.
When you're on a hike
And you're on your bike.
When night comes the moonlight shines.
When stars are out
You shout.

In the Rainforest
by Maddi Carter

Monkeys swing in the trees,
Snakes rustle in the leaves,
Birds chirping in the sky,
Dragonflies fly up high,
Squirrels make their nests,
Flies are being such pests,
Spiders crawling on the ground,
So much nature all around.

Forest Tour
by Jackson Frewin

Snakes are slithering on the floor.
Little mice are climbing up to their mother's door.
Chipmunks all eating nuts, thinking it's fall.
Bumblebees sticking to the wall.
The hawk says all the mice are staying indoors.
Bunnies all jumping on the forest floors.
Butterflies all flying in the breeze.
All the animals are saying please!

Animals I See
by Brady McHenry

Bears are catching fish in the lake.
Deer are standing still to look fake.
Birds are flying in the sky.
Chipmunks are chewing acorns as if it's pie.
Beavers are building with twigs.
Rabbits, they like to dig.
Snakes are slithering on the ground.
Squirrels are hiding, nowhere to be found.

Titanic
by Erik Nolasco

The people suffered
It killed about 1,500 people including kids
The ship is at the bottom of the ocean
An iceberg was the cause of the sinking
No men were allowed on the lifeboats
Its destination was New York
Carpathia, a ship, rescued the survivors

Hedgehog War
by Paul Garofalo

Little hedgehog marches up the hill.
His rifle slung over his shoulder.
With all his might he climbs over boulders.
He is ready to fight. Even if limbs are sore,
He will not back down from war.
He sees enemies up ahead,
He makes to run but instead
He raises his rifle and BOOM, fume arises from the gun,
He missed but now the enemies are on the run.

Loved
by Beatriz Hernandez Guerrero

Love is a strong word
Love means treating people with respect, kindness
and having positive thoughts
When you do all that, your heart feels fuzzy and warm.
Love also means when you meet somebody,
in your heart you feel like he/she is the one.
Awww! Love, isn't it beautiful.
But I'm not finished yet.
Love also means treating your parents with it
and your parents also treating you with it.
Like me, I might be poor but I have my family with me.
They love me.
I love them.
So this is the only thing I want to tell you.
Fill the world with love, it's not that hard.
"wink"

Gymnastics
by Lexi Adamson

Girls and boys flip and tumble
Yearn to go to the Olympics
Medals to win
Needle kicks on beam
A way to be active
Stretching before practice
Trophies to win
In the gymnastics room, gymnasts flip
Cartwheels all over the place
Splits when stretching

Express Bus Esophagus
by Ella Holmstrom

I needed to take a trip to Acid Lane
I really didn't want to because I knew it would be a pain
I hopped on the Express Bus
Which I soon found out it was like my Esophagus.
Along the way there were some bumps
Some were small but some felt like big lumps
All of a sudden came this big loud rush of wind
That nearly sent us flying up into a tailspin.
Thankfully the bus straightened out
And so it gives me nothing more to talk about
I am glad to report that we have reached our destination to our Acid Lane run
So long folks, we are finally done.

Caution
by Alana Dillon

In an imaginary land far, far, away I woke up to the break of day.
I walked into the woods to see where my imagination would take me.
And, oh! What a beautiful sight I was blessed to see!
Piles of gold, silver, and more all just in the woods to store.
All just stacked so delicately, I wondered if it caused vanity.
An advisable man walked by. And oh, did he let out a great sigh!
"For I am poor," said the man, "I only want money in a small can."
I walked over to him and said,
"You can have some of my treasure. Now would you, friend?"
He grabbed it all to keep, and let out a great leap.
The money turned into rubbish in a keep.
And there I was, left alone to weep.

Summer
by Jason Jordan Lopez

Summer
Fun, Hot
Swimming, Playing, Biking
Spending time with family
Camping, Canoeing, Gardening
Calm, Free
Season

Oceans
by Matthew Amend

When I traveled the ocean,
There was no commotion,
Sometimes not even a motion,
In the ocean there are so many sights to see,
In my boat I just let everything be,
So many things to see for me,
When it's time to go I leave and tell of all things you will find,
I want go to the ocean again, just rewind!

Spring
by Ananya Balachander

Warm rays of sunshine trickle through,
the branches of trees, freshly blossoming,
their silhouettes reflected,
in the sweet waters of the bubbling brook.
This world is oh so sweet, we must cherish it.
The quiet meadow is now full,
with new life,
for every animal has had a long rest,
and each awaits a new beginning.
Happy chirps fill the air,
along with the fragrant smell of earth,
like rain over jasmine.
This world is oh so sweet, we must cherish it.
New bursts of color,
through the open meadow,
the sky an exhilarating blue,
for there's nothing we can do,
to not enjoy this,
This world is oh so sweet, we must cherish it.

My Baby Sister
by Thomas Hart

I love my baby sister
even though she can barely speak.
I love all of the little noises she makes.
And I especially love when she walks around
with all crooked steps.
That is why I love my baby sister.

The Turtles
by Hannah Nicklay

The turtles all around me.
While I'm sitting by a tree.
It was just like it was meant for me!
The turtles are dancing 'round.
The sun was just bound to find me!
It was just like it was meant to be!
For once, the turtles came.
I finally claimed they were mine.
It turns out, that was kinda lame.
The sun went to sleep,
I guess I should too.
I found a clue to help you.
Goodnight.
See you in the daylight.

Country Sights
by Abigail Bauer

Running with the wind in my hair,
breathing in the fresh country air,
Stopping and listening,
Watching the dew glistening,
Sneaking upon the fox,
Who is basking on the rocks,
I start stalking the deer,
Who is perking his ears,
Start running again,
And see the wolf in her den,
Running past the creek,
Looking for something to seek,
What more to seek,
When running by the creek,
Than running with the wind in my hair,
Breathing the fresh country air.

Cave In the Deep
by Amelia Lane-Outlaw

You are deep in a cave full of rock, how are you in shock,
Deep in the Alps where you live,
Stalactites and stalagmites are creeping on the ceilings and floors,
Mites crawling on you from head to toe, from fright to love,
This is how life goes.

God
by Katherine Andrade

God, my Dear Lord.
I pray every night while thinking of You.
Knowing how much You care and think of us too!
The next day feeling safe knowing that You're with me too!
How You sacrificed Your life to make us live.
I don't know how to thank You!
But the only thing I can say is, I love You and thank You for life and family.
I love You

Spring
by Teagen Van Lith

The green grass waves at me
The dancing raindrops dance in the rain
The bright colorful flowers wave in the wind
The trees grow leaves on the long branches
The big green leaves grow on the branches
The tall green grass waves in the wind

Writing For the Fun of It
by Avery Maltese

When you write a sentence there is always a period at the end,
that is just the way it is.
The only reason is because that is how we learned it.
That is officially what is right. But why?
I thought you could write any way you think is right and wouldn't it be?

Look and see:
I Can WRiTe Anyway i feel is Fit,
buT can u unDerStAnd iT?

Life taught us it this way for reasons we may not know.
And for these reasons there is a period at the end of this sentence
and a capital letter to start a new one.
But trust me and try to write just for the fun of it.

Day and Night
by Audrey Hentges

Sun
Bright, Hot
Blinding, Scorching, Warming
Sun stays still; Moon has phases
Rotating, Following, Reflecting
Dark, Phases
Moon

My Baby Brother
by Mackenzie Flowers

He always drools.
He always coos at me.
He always clicks his tongue.
He always helps himself up.
He always acts cute.
He always tries to crawl.
He always loves baby food.
He always makes a big mess.
He always likes to cuddle.
He always tries to climb.
He always loves hugs and kisses.
He always has messy hair.
He always is so adorable.
He always plays with toys.
He always begs for chips.
He always laughs at me.
He always tries to hug me.
He always pulls my hair.
He always loves piggyback rides.
He always loves to be loved.
He always loves fruits and veggies.
He always teethes on his toys.
He always loves my beads.
He always loves pretty much every time I play with him.

3rd Place

Kayla Childs

Ladybug
by Kayla Childs

Captivating patterns.
Tiny legs cling to emerald green blades of grass,
Hoping to find a morsel to eat.
Stepping cautiously into the light,
Its delicate wings like stained glass windows,
Deciding that it is time to find a new home.
Black spots winking at the sun,
One of millions but different ...
Lifts ever so fragile wings,
and flies away,
Like he was never there.

2nd Place

Trishika Chintakunta

Hunger
by Trishika Chintakunta

Dripping delicacies swam in my vision,
The monster inside me was gnawing relentlessly at my conscience,
It felt like I was paralyzed,
The knots keeping me together slowly unraveled.
Blonde ringlets cascaded down her face
as she stared dreamily at her snack.
I sprinted over to the girl, my cold hands wrestling hers for the food,
Victory was mine.
They say fortune favors the bold but I am a coward.
To me light is a distant dream,
So I hide in the darkness.
Eating the food, the monster was satisfied,
But something that should taste like Heaven,
Tasted like misery.

1st Place

Finn Ramnarain

Having already won awards for some of his short stories,
Finn decided to try his hand at poetry
after being inspired by a memorable visit to a holocaust museum.
In addition to creative writing,
this talented fifth grader also enjoys soccer and photography.
In his spare time, Finn loves to be outdoors,
with the beach being one of his favorite places.
Great work, Finn!

Szymon's Last Dream
by Finn Ramnarain

I dreamt of you last night, Mama
you were singing as you made our dinner.
The smell of bread filled the air
and you laughed when my stomach rumbled.
You held me in my dream, Mama
we were safe and happy at home.
The yellow stars were twinkling in the sky
and we were free to be ourselves.
This morning when I woke up
I remembered you were gone, Mama.
The only bread I have is moldy
and my stomach never stops rumbling.
Our lives mean nothing to these soldiers
we are German but we are Jews.
This morning when I woke up
I knew I would see you soon, Mama.
The time for dreams is over
I do not want to wake up here again.

Division II

Grades 6-7

What Happened?
by Ashley Radman

When we would play we had a great time
When we would talk we went to other places
When we would be together it felt like I was complete.
But now you have left me alone
But now you have moved away
But now you don't play.
I grew up with you
I grew up without you
I grew up reserved.
You still come over sometimes
You still play with me
You still talk to me.
But when you are not around I feel broken
But when you are not around I feel incomplete
But when you are not around I feel like I am on the edge.
We used to say everything that came to our minds
We used to play anything that we thought was fun
We used to laugh at every little thing that would happen.
But not anymore.
You left me alone, but I forgive you.

Books
by Julia Toenyan

Books
Happy, special
Reading, laughing, amazing
It makes you feel special.
Fictional

Glimmers of Hope
by Abby Powers

The pain of choice goes so deep
Trying to get to the surface for air
The searching splitting me in two
When you rise you plummet back down
No air to breathe in the bottoms of decisions
When pulling you out they slip with you
Getting pulled down deeper and deeper as you go
When suddenly you see the light of hope
Dangling by the last thread it pulls you up
You reach the surface gasping for air
It lets you see a world of happiness
Giving you a chance to live with no worries

Big Red
by Quentin Van Dam

He is a big tractor
He does a lot of big jobs
He does planting, cultivating, and ripping
He has not a whole lot of power
But he has a great job
And a great owner

Beautiful Things ...
by Amarianna Vinje

The most beautiful things in life can come from the strangest places.
They aren't always in the easiest places
that's why you may have difficulty finding them.
Beautiful things such as the amount of love someone can have all in one's heart,
or how a simple smile can brighten a person's entire day.
The smallest things can make the biggest difference in life.
Most people tend to take these wonderful notions for granted.
The most beautiful thing in life is knowing that people have the ability
to love one another unconditionally.
Think of all the endless love we share, and maybe, just maybe,
life won't seem as though everything is in despair.

God's Beat
by Kathryn Prins

When I lay down and rest,
I feel my heart beating in my chest.
I know that God is keeping the steady beat
To the many measures of my life.
Whether the song is loud or soft,
Accented, choppy, or smooth going,
I know that I am not alone.
When my song is over,
When my race is run,
When my heart stops beating,
I know that it is done.
Through a simple heartbeat,
It makes many musical ways,
Through a simple heartbeat,
I live all of my days.

Praise be to God, the Father of all!
Even the smallest heartbeat can make a whole world of difference!

English
by Madisen Stillwell

English is a class
that almost everyone can pass
There is the noun
a noun could be a town
There is punctuation
for each type of communication
English is fun
it will make your mind run

Success
by Grace Matthiesen

Sitting there wondering
How high you can achieve
Maybe mountains high
Or as much as a little worn down hill
In my own words a mountain is like success
Or achieving very high
Everybody has their own mountain high
As high as they can get it
Believe you can climb high
Everybody can climb their own distance

Cowgirls
by Anastasia Hines

I think of myself as a cowgirl,
Sitting in an oyster being the pearl,
Different than the others,
Brave, and cute say the mothers,
My pig is my best friend,
I always have a carrot to lend,
Rolling around in the odor filled mud,
Like putting chocolate icing on my bud,
I learned the language of pigs,
I don't care if I look odd to other kids,
We go together like peanut butter and jelly,
But my pig has a very chubby belly,
I think of us like cowgirls,
Sitting in an oyster being the pearls,
Different than the others,
Stinky and pinky say the brothers.

T-Rex
by Lance Anderson

A giant footstep from a tremendous beast.
It's larger than an elephant, as long as a school bus
with teeth as long as bananas.
Its big roar can be heard from miles away.
As it wakes up, it's searching for food.
As it finds its favorite meal, it starts chasing the giant reptiles with three horns.
As it devours the flesh the sun is setting.
It heads home after a very long day.

Grandpa
by Jack Koranda

This is my grandpa.
He works with wood.
He played with me
He loved me.
The outdoors is sunshine.
We play baseball.
While my dad is in the shed.
and the trees are growing.

Untitled
by Jenna Toftum

I miss those days
When everything was perfect
Emma, Charlize, and me
Best pals
It makes me feel happy, calm and old
Everything so nice
They were there for my birthday parties and sleepovers
I wish I was a little kid again
We were always so bright
We were still in a pose, happy
There were so many colors
Charlize's yellow shirt, my purple dress to Emma's red shirt
So sad, I wish we could go back in time
Everything was perfect
I miss being that young
I miss those days

Ugly
by Kathryn Redning

Slippery, squirmy, electric bite,
My blood boiling.
Pale, fleshy, pink,
The fake, horrid smell right from its home.
The stench sears my eyes.
Poppy, shrill, horrible sound.
Chewy, fleshy, disgusting taste,
An inhuman cry, the flash of a blade.

Loser, a Sad Story
by Kyler Wiese

Once upon a time there was a boy who had no friends
he got bullied a lot, all he wanted was friends but no one listened
then one of the bullies punched him in the face
then a person came over and told the bully to stop and the bullies listened
and that person became friends with him, then they got married and had kids
they lived in a penthouse in New York but one day
the bullies tracked them down and came to their house
but they didn't expect them to say sorry
from everything they did to them.

Remember When
by Danielle Dickey

I remember when you used to chew on your toys,
Laying down on the couch, chewing in peace.
It was cold outside ... we had to keep you in.
But why don't you chew your toys anymore?
I remember when we first got you,
You were barking and jumping up and down.
Kirby just standing by, not wanting to greet us.
But why don't you jump up and down like you used to?
I remember when you are naughty,
You always bite me or my brother,
And we put you in the kennel for a while.
But why do you always bite me or my brother?
I remember when I get home from school,
You come running toward me
And bending down on my knees so I can hug you.
But why are you always tied up now?

The Beach
by Maggie Roscher

Beach sand tickles my toes,
Warm summer air twitches my nose.
Clear blue water splashes my feet,
Sound of an ice cream truck makes me crave something sweet.
Kids play, laugh and run,
While I lay down in the burning hot sun.
The beach is the place I want to be,
I hope someday that I'll never leave.

Last Moment
by Hailey Kircher

I remember when we were outside
playing fetch.
Why did you stop returning it to me?
I remember when you
would lay by our beds
You would sleep anywhere.
Why didn't you wake up?
I remember how you acted
you couldn't hear
but you always knew.
Do you remember me?

The Flyer
by Dallas Hanks

Once upon a time there was a boy
He was an average boy that you see in a run-down town runnin' around
Then one day he finally explored the town
Then he got lost
And then he found out
The whole time he was lost he had been actually found
He found his true home
He knew this 'cuz he fit in with the others
Then he started runnin' out of fuel and crashed back
So he kept doing what he did that one special day
He wasn't lucky the first few weeks
Then finally he went to his new home for a grip like every other day
He'd have so much fun up there
So he kept going
And he finally got what he needed
And that was the top

The River
by Tiffany Johnson

Quiet as a bird's chirp
Flowing in the wind like grass
The river flows on

Family
by Madeline Oliff

Family are the people that you love and cherish
With all of your heart
Sometimes you might hate each other or be mad at each other
But at the end of the day you're still family
Family is more than just your friends
They are the people who will always be with you
They are the people who care about you more than anything
Family are the people that you are supposed to trust but some don't
Family are the people that you love
For the rest of your life
Life is short
So live all of it with your family

Time To Fly Away
by Taylor McCoy

As the flowers bloom,
As the trees blossom,
Sit below your willow.
Dear child- sit below,
Let the birds fly away.
As the stars take flight,
As the moon in sight,
Let your body be so.
Dear young adult- sit below,
Let the birds fly away.
As the children play,
As the churchmen say,
Let your thoughts and age grow.
Dear adult- sit below,
Let the birds fly away.
As the sad goodbyes,
As the baby cries,
Sit below your willow.
Dear grandparent- sit below,
Let yourself fly away and rest below your willow.

Ms. Tinawi
by Jennie Pavon Peralta

Ms. Tinawi
Smart, funny
Singing, dancing, teaching
Smile on her face
Smiling, sharing, amazing
Beautiful, kind
Teacher

I Believe
by Layton Johnston

I believe in Jesus Christ
I believe in forgiving people for mistakes
I believe everybody is loved
I believe you can find happiness in the smallest of things
I believe everybody has a place in this world
I believe everybody has something
I believe family and love is everything

20 Lines
by Quinci Larson

20 lines is all I'm given,
To explain how badly I need to be forgiven.
Not because I want to,
Trust me, if I didn't need to touch the door handle 15 times,
No, 16 times in one day if it's Wednesday
Do you see what I'm trying to convey?
Because my OCD is a buffet, and I need to get away.
But my urge to check, and re-check, and re-re-check the door handle 15 times,
no 16 times, is like my stomach, it only gets bigger.
People tell me I only gain weight because I overeat because of stress,
But no one knows that I didn't ask for my stress, or anxiety, or any of it.
It's all a package I can't get rid of.
Obsessive-compulsive disorder. Huh, see that's not what anyone told me it meant,
Except, for me it meant overly complicated daughter.
But I didn't write to you to talk about how I check things
or how I worry about how we'll all die.
I wrote to apologize, to you, Mom and Dad,
I'm sorry I'm not the perfect daughter, and I'm sorry I'm a mistake,
But I really hope you will enjoy the peace
in the fact that I'm no longer your daughter.

Friends ...
by Savannah Kent

Having friends is ridiculous, all the lies and talks they have.
I for one know this.
I was friends with two very close people, they cast me aside
and left me afloat until I sunk when I heard their lies.
My life turned upside down that day.
I saw them everywhere and couldn't escape.
I'm still trapped. Even when I'm alone, I'm still trapped.
We gave each other nicknames, we used them all the time.
I loved it. Now every time I hear them I try not to puke.
All the times I saved them from a stupid bouncing ball, they said "thanks."
Now I wish I would have left them to get hit in the face.
I tried to hide the pain from them.
But every time I did they seem to make a mess.
I can't hide from them, I know this.
I don't run, I don't hide. I talk to other friends as I walk by.
The group I have now has accepted me in,
but I still have dreams of all the memories.
I am hurt, I'm in pain but I don't hide it.
I show them I'm not afraid even when I grieve.
I'm alone ... but I am brave.

Equality
by Zachary Byers

You judge us based on skin,
and don't try to know us.
You make us not fit in,
and throw us under the bus.
Why do you put us down,
when we don't believe the same as you do.
You want us to frown,
because we are not like you.
You cut us with your eyes,
and insult us with your words.
You write books full of lies,
and make others' visions blurred.
You are not any better
than the ones that you hate.
Still you think you are greater,
than the ones you separate.
One day I hope we will be together,
and be treated the same.
One day I know life will be better
than this century filled with shame.

Your Kind
by Sarah Azam

Your kind does not belong here
Sit in the back of the bus
Your kind does not belong here
You will never fit in with us
Your kind does not belong here
You don't pour the same tears and sweat
Your kind does not belong here
The darker you are, the lesser you get
But where do my rights come from in this place?
The dark in my heart,
Or the dark on my face?
Who knew I could be owned like an item
Merely because of my race
Your kind does not belong here
You won't be given rights or power
Your kind does not belong here
Because your skin is not like ours

Nobody Knows Why
by Kyla Donner

Rumors. I don't know
Why people have to spread rumors
Maybe it's for attention
Or they don't want people to know the truth ... whatever it is.
It's really hard, when you lose a friend
And you don't know why he's gone.
But instead of telling
People that we don't
Know why he's gone ...
They still have
To spread rumors.
"He was being bullied." "He was going blind."
"He was having trouble in school." "Family issues."
I'm sick of these lies.
It hurts me
It hurts his family
It hurts his friends.
Nobody knows for sure why he is gone,
and people need to wake up and realize that
Before they get hurt like the rest of us
We're all like blue balloons drifting through the air
Sad.

The Owl
by Amelia Smith

The owl flies through the night
Silently
With the moon on his wings
Then off of the tree
His mate takes flight
Together
The owls fly silently through the night

The Beginning of Winter
by Mae Nephew

The bird is perched up in the tree.
While we rest on the bench by the apple tree.
There are yellow, pink, and red apples too.
They're not yet ripe, but good for you.
While the leaves fall from the autumn trees,
the breeze blows them so close to me.
The breeze makes me shiver.
While the old bush starts to wither,
and that's what I call the beginning of winter.

Horses
by Alexis Schroer

People say
Horses were made on the breath
Of the wind,
And the beauty of the angel.
Horses will be with me for the rest of my days.
Though, when my last moment has come and gone,
I know I won't have my last breath with them.
But I do know I will be with my Sonny
In his last moments,
Even if I pray every night that I'll have
Him with me every day.
I know that like everything we love,
We have to let go.
Even though that time will be the hardest,
Most painful moment of my life.
I will know that I will see him again
Where there is no pain or sadness,
And no hurting.
We will be together forever.
Inseparable.

Remember When
by MJ Lunde

I remember when I was on that plane
I had a face of excitement
It was a cold winter day
But why was it so warm in Florida
I remember when I saw Disney World
It was so cool and awesome at the same time
My sister was amazed as I was
I don't know why there is so many rides
I remember when I saw my cousin
That I only see 1-2 times per year
First thing we did was going swimming
I have no idea why I swam so long

Friends
by Ayva Jackson

Friends only last so long ...
All your secrets you tell each other ...
All the special moments ...
All the sleepovers you shared ...
All the dumb inside jokes ...
They all start to fade ...
Your friendship starts to fall apart ...
You hope they want your friendship back ...
But they probably don't ...
You want to tell them sorry ...
But you're too scared ...
To tell them one word ...
"I'm sorry ..."
Then your friendship is over ...

I Believe
by Riki LaTour

I believe that everyone makes mistakes and it's ok
I believe that everything happens for a reason
and even when it's rough at times there is always a happy ending
I believe horse abuse and animal is NEVER ok
I believe that if you keep dreaming the same dream it's bound to happen
I believe everyone has freedom of speech but should use it correctly
I believe that bullying to an extreme amount should be illegal
I believe that the people who fight for our country should have more rights
I believe everyone should be treated equally
I believe

It Is What It Is
by Maddy Hanson

Life, sad, gloomy, melancholy
Elated, exhilarated, ecstatic
It is a fruit that is sweet and bitter at the same time.
Death always haunts your shadows,
but you manage to outrun it or it comforts you.
It is a trap that many know and few see.
Though sad, it is the reason for existence.
Longevity denies the truth and medicines further you from the truth.
Though we know it, we never know when it will happen.
Many sorrow for death, but embracing it is acceptance.
Life is a journey, and death is the end.
The end of your journey is the beginning of a new one.
This is life.
And it is what it is.

Enslaved I Lie
by Kamrin Iverson

As the wind flew by
Still here– enslaved I lie
Lie like the lilacs, lie like the trees, lie like the cool, fresh, summer breeze
As the Earth may come to ease
Still here– enslaved I lie
Stuck in this world of cruelty, stuck in this world of pain,
never show my face in public
Because I am attached to this chain, as my heart dreams of flying high
Still here– enslaved I lie
Dreams of the daisies, dream of the wood, dream of the timber–
wishing I could
Still here– enslaved I lie
I am cemented to this piece of metal, I am fastened to this steel
If only I could take control, and learn to steer the wheel
I dream of moving mountain rocks, but– they never move
Still here– enslaved I lie
Move out of this chain, get out of this lane
Still here– enslaved I lie
I wish I were allowed to fly, but I am still here, being puzzled together
Still here– enslaved I lie
Lie like the river, lie like the bees, just trying to find the right type of: Key.
Still here– enslaved I lie

Why So ...
by Madison Paal

Why so dismal? Hiding in the dust,
A once strong woman now starting to rust.
Feeling defeated, always in a worry.
Never feeling safe, constantly in a hurry
Our ancestors fought to get us here today.
So we need to do that for others and their days.
The change might not be now, but like good cheese
It gets better as the days go on
Why so confused? Can't all be great.
In a once happy world now everyone is like fresh bait
Wishing to help, but nothing can be done.
Unless we all fight united as one
If we all stick together, quit singing these sad songs
And shout for what's right. It's not just about the words
That come deep in our hearts, but the affect they will have.
Like a blooming flower to one's rainy day
Why so joyful? Leaping with lust.
No more are our rights collecting dust.
For we– strong– people, never gave up!
Although we won, we are never done

I Think
by Kylie Larson

I lie here, and I wonder.
I wonder, I wonder
I think of all the times when it was just happy endings
I remember, I remember
I think everything is going to be okay when it's over
I think, I think
I think I'll wanna keep going when the darkness sets in,
I think, I think
I think that everyone will be with me when I have no one else
I hope, I hope
I think that I'll make it through and everything will be just fine
I think, I think
I think that the time will never come for when the world falls apart
I think, I think
I think nothing is happening when the sky starts falling down
shedding tears and crushing dreams
I think, I think
I think everything will always be the same
I think, I think, I think

Sky
by Josselin Cardenas

Shine on all people
The sky is full of colors
All types of weather

Taking a Step Further Away
by Gabrielle Wills

Trees, trees, trees,
Everywhere I look,
Colorful, crispy leaves staring at me,
Morning dew sprinkling over green grass,
Getting pushed down every step taken
Towards my unknown destination
Springing back up every time I take a step away,
Away from my past,
Rain washing away all my worries, regrets,
Taking me away,
Every step I'm getting farther and farther away from the past
At the end of the journey there's light,
Lighting up my future

Equality
by Ally Carlson

I lie here
Wishing and hoping.
One day I know
We will all live peacefully together.
But for now
We live in a world full of hatred and darkness.
One day I say.
One day.
But for now
Our hope for peace, is like a balloon drifting away on a windy day.
But we try, try to jump up and catch it.
One day I say.
One day.
One day we will jump up and finally reach it.
Everyone will sit.
And be happy.
Because we are all equal.
And we live together in harmony.
Today I say.
It has to be today.

Summer Nights
by Channy Johnson

Waves crash quietly
Sun shining bright at the beach
Stars glow, sand sparkles

Best Friend
by Kaylee Gale

Her smile is as bright as
the sun on steroids.
Her self-discipline soccer skills are
good as gold. She laughs like
Nobody is watching, ahaa!
Her happiness is contagious as chicken pox.
She makes my problems, her problems.
She is supportive like the Earth, because
I couldn't live without her.
Her personality is what truly makes
her my best friend.

I've Got a Secret
by Brielle Peterman

I've got a secret
for the deep
the ones who have trouble
falling asleep
I've got a secret
for the sad
the ones who feel pain
that just demands to be had
I've got a secret
for the weak
the ones who feel small
in the eyes of the peak
And I've got a secret
for the mad
maybe everything won't turn out
oh so bad
I've got a secret
That in times that seem to go bad
It'll all be okay
Some days just have to be had.

Autumn
by Kareena Ferguson

Leaves slip quietly
Fall is around the corner
The air gets colder

Hope
by Jacob Reininger

Hope
Always rising, always falling
Hope
Running like a rabbit, fighting like a wolf
Hope
Bonding like a dream
Dividing like a wall
Hope
Building the greatest cities
Destroying the greatest empires
Hope
Moving mountains
Hope
Never there
Never gone
Hope

Someday
by Ashley Therrien

We treat them like animals with no way out,
We think we can control them and shout,
We think we can just kick them out,
Someday
We stomp on them like they're a walkway,
We think they will always obey,
We think their hope will just decay,
Someday
We punish them with no way out,
We think they will go about,
We think they are just in doubt,
Someday
Someday our separation will be broken
Someday we all will be one
Someday we will stop hoping
Someday this will all be done.

Before the River Froze
by Kayla Meeks

I remember when the water used to flow
It was like a drifting feather.
The sun would burst.
But why? Why are you just a sheet of ice now?
I remember when you used to take me with your current.
It was like summer not ending.
I knew that summer was near its end.
But what made you want to be so cold?
I remember when I used to skip rocks on you.
It was like magic.
The shiny water.
Why don't you stay water forever?

Dream
by Catie Lowe

Once I was a child with much belief
Then one person said follow your dream
So I got some paper
And gathered my pens
Then I stayed up writing until half past ten
I stayed up writing until the moon came out and stars began to shine
I smiled to myself
I wrote and wrote and then the ink ran out
I wrote and the fountain pen began to spout
But hidden away in a library today
Is the work that I made
A poem called Dream

I Believe
by Erin Uecker

I believe ...
I believe that everyone should be treated equally.
I believe that even if you feel down you don't have to feel down forever.
I believe that everyone has gifts and they should not be afraid of them.
I believe heroes are the ones you love.
I believe that even if you don't like someone you still have to be nice to them.
I believe you always have to forgive even if you don't want to.
I believe that kindness is better than money.
I believe no matter what you dream
it will always come true if you work hard to do it.
I believe ...

Thanksgiving
by Madison Carsten

Everyone sitting together
Giving thanks
Eating big feasts
Pouring a stream of gravy
That flows into a
Lake in your mashed potatoes
Like a river rushing into
An ocean

I Believe
by Jolie Uecker

I believe there is a world with no sickness.
I believe people can find a way.
I believe our world can become a better place.
I believe everybody can change the world.
I believe people are kind even if they don't show it.
I believe a friend will hate you, but if you do something to connect
you two again, you can be friends again.
I believe you might fall down but if you fall down, I believe you can get back up.
I believe if someone breaks your heart, there is someone to fix it.

Waterfall
by Ellie Sorensen

The waterfall calls out to me,
Flowing into the shining sea.
It whispers to the sparkling shells,
It declares its story to tell.
The water murmurs in my ear,
So soft that I can barely hear.
As the wind rustles through the trees,
And laughs quietly in the breeze.
Underneath the glistening sea,
The sea creatures swim silently.
The dolphins dive beneath the shore,
The otters laugh and beg for more.
The sun slowly sets to the west,
The moon will soon be at its best.
The stars are growing very bright,
All is calm as it becomes night.

My Bad Dream
by Taylor Mauser

One night I woke up from a bad dream.
I really wanted to shout and scream.
I wanted to call Mom,
Instead of waking Tom.
But then I got up and had ice cream.

Summer
by Genevieve Kopp

Spears of sun shatter the glass windows,
Racing through the hallway,
Orphaning all of your past misery of a slave to the clock,
Free once more from its malevolence.
You hear cheers and shouts
And the wave of excitement devours you whole,
The wind singing in harmony with the school's final bell ringing.

Dakota: The Treaties of 1851
by Cooper Olson

They wanted our land
Our land we lived on for they demand
The giant herds of buffalo we hunt
Cannot even feed a runt
We kill no game
Which is a shame
Our horses are as thin
As the chances that we may win
Our dogs are lean
And the white men are mean
You think it's a good deal
But it's really a steal
The treaty will be the best they say
But they really just want to push us out of the way
The money is small so we are glad
But we are still a little mad
I touch a pen, a pen that gives up land
They take the land because of the public's great demand
We are the Great Dakota
But we may never again roam the plains of Minnesota

Room Cleaning
by Sabrina Sterrett

Imagine a room dark and grim,
the switch is on but light is slim.
A sight of destruction meets your eyes,
worse than a tornado whizzing by –
books and papers stuffed everywhere,
pens, pencils, Post-its, high in the air,
piles of clothes and trash, it's true;
your mind is whirling, what to do?
Suddenly, something flies past your ear,
a book, or a pencil, what was there?
Then rulers and scissors twirl with glee;
they swoop and dive in harmony.
Clean clothes jump up and begin to dance
into their drawers and closet expanse.
Pretty soon the whole floor is bare,
my rug is vacuumed, without a stray hair.
The room looks so clean that I think to myself:
the tremendous mess must have cleaned itself.

Alone
by Madison Kiniry

I have known how it feels
Alone during lunchtime again
See the people walk by
You feel invisible and scared
No one notices you
You close your eyes and start to cry
You curl into a ball
The feeling of nothing in you
Have no one by your side
Those people say hi and smile
But nothing will help you
For you know they do not really care
You wish someone were here
Sadness fills your heart and your soul
The sadness can stop you
You feel you can't do anything
Have no one to lean on
I see you at lunch all alone
I have come to say "Hi".
See I have come to be your friend, and never let you down!

Perception Is Everything
by Julia LeBlanc

Refusing to escape her confined state of mind,
so open to disappointment, so fixated on her own faults.
Believing that any mark is her world's undoing.
Endlessly examining every angle, every possible view.
Perception is everything.
Navigating through an infinite labyrinth of emotions.
Eyes locked on her own reflection, disgusted with who stares back.
Self hatred fuels the pounding in her chest.
Perception is everything.
Craving the irresistible feeling of safety that only isolation can provide.
Lifeless hair streaming down the sides of her gaunt face.
Acne peppered across her pallid skin.
Haunted by her thoughts ... never enough.
Perception is everything.
The walls that were once comforting, now suffocating.
The mirror's glare blinded her judgment, mentally filtering her view.
A sudden jagged crack, spreading through the reality she once believed.
Self worth, an unknown concept fearfully taking its first steps.
Is perception everything?

What I've Learned In 2 and a Half Years
by Soeun Lee

You may not understand this poem, but if you are a human,
not an android, you will understand. Humans can understand
because they have a kind mind, heart, and soul.
I tried to hide myself, tried to be like an android without a heart,
mind, and soul, just trying to be like other humans or animals.
I just didn't know how amazing I am already,
how special, how unique, and how much loved.
My home was now across the ocean, so I didn't want to be here
and fit in where I thought I belonged.
But I knew this was my home now, and I needed to fit in.
But it was hard. I was afraid of being left alone, laughed at,
and ignored just because I'm a bit different.
"Everyone is different and special, and has different powers.
These are what made them "them"," I knew this fact, but many didn't.
Years went by, now I know I don't have to hide myself in a box
and just cry. I learned another fact: you don't have to be something
or someone that you are not and the "you" you don't belong to.
Be yourself. Don't care about what other mean people around you say-
they just don't know the fact. Love people by who they are inside,
love who they are, not their appearance.
I know this fact is already in everyone's mind,
but this fact, you gotta know it in your heart.

The Wind
by Sophia Camacho

The wind was whipping around us
Like snakes slithering around our ankles
You never see it coming until it strikes
It coils around you because it is sly
And you do not see it as it passes by.

A Walk Through Thorns
by Jacob Downs

Through the thorns I trudged on
waiting and waiting for the dawn.
As I felt the cuts of the thorns
I was not thinking about my mourns.
As the bear came closer and closer
I was not to be his proposer.
When dawn comes a little more
it will be time for me to settle the score.
Then dawn struck the sky
it was time to unleash my battle cry.
Coming forward to fight
I knew I had to do this right.
As the bear drew closer to me
I knew I had a way to flee.
I trapped the bear in the thorns
there is where his spirit lay torn.

I Believe
by Brianna McClanahan

I believe–
I believe happiness comes in the simplest of things.
I believe love is in everything you will ever see.
I believe you can only be yourself because everyone else is already taken.
I believe everyone you will ever look at has plenty of room for improvement.
I believe crying isn't always bad.
I believe change can be a very good and bad thing in life but it must happen.
I believe music is a form of emotion and is good for the soul.
I believe every child deserves a happy and amazing life.
I believe reading is a language of feelings and thoughts.
I believe perfection isn't real.

A+
by Dohee Lee

Tapping on my desk,
alternating my fingers from my pinky to thumb,
I wait until a white piece of paper is on the surface.
My heart skips a beat.
For the first time,
I see a big, red, A+ on the right corner of the paper.
Beside it is a name, a name I don't recognize
"Oops! That's mine!"
a voice says as my smile fades away

Fishing and Hunting
by Lane Hoefs

Hunting,
The big bucks shot,
Up at the crack of dawn,
The glow of the sky in morning,
Silence,
Fishing,
The cast at dusk,
The big fish that are caught,
The fishing stories that are fun,
The peace,
The fun,
The peace and quiet,
The critters on the go,
The strange noises heard beneath the stand,
The peace

Aiyana and Jonathan
by Andrew Melanson

Aiyana
Aiyana's mind, which is unable to fathom the approaching ships, is curious
Watching from the shore, she cannot foresee her impotent destiny
Her placidity is delightfully contagious
Aiyana, who is not afraid of the imperative changes to come,
is hopeful for her future.
Jonathan
Jonathan's journey across the sea of darkness,
which caused impotency to invade his heart, is coming to an end
The final moments approaching the shore were made placid by his faith in God
Imperatively placed cannons insure his safety
Jonathan, whose mind could not fathom the statement "Welcome English",
is hopeful for his future

Listening
by Ellie Ludwig

Listening, nothing is there, I can only hear the sound of the wind blowing,
I sit there, listening, waiting for something to happen
The sound of the bees and the trees is a distant reminder of that day,
The day that I could never forget,
The day with no joy,
I am fighting a battle for my life every day,
what will happen next, I do not know,
but I first must travel this long dark road.

Peace Or Hate?
by Ella Countryman

Do you ever wonder what would happen if the world was at peace?
What would happen if everyone was polite to each other?
Would we be too kind -
like telling each other that the other person can go first?
Would we be too kind and not be able to be strict to children?
But what if there was only hate in the world?
Where no one cared about anyone,
People shoving, pushing, fighting, stealing,
and putting more kids into slavery?
What if everybody just stopped and thought
about too much hate or too much peace,
What if we didn't stop hatred and didn't stop peace?
Would the world be at its best position?
Then that gets you thinking ... about who cares and who doesn't?
Would we be able to know right from wrong and still have no peace?
All of this is just a thought
Or is it reality?

I Believe
by Anna McClelland

I believe that no matter how hard you try, life will never be fair.
I believe that you need to work for good things, not ask for them.
I believe that you shouldn't make fun of people,
because you don't know everyone's story.
I believe that if you try hard enough, you will get somewhere in life.
I believe that everyone is an equal, so they should be treated like one.
I believe that if one wants peace, don't go and ruin it.
I believe that love trumps hate, but people don't realize that.
I believe that crying is ok, and everyone does it, so don't be scared to let it out.
I believe that sometimes you need to get your hands a little dirty.
I believe that no man is made of steel.
I believe.

3 Ways of Looking At Life
by Adrianna Gaspard

Life is like a bowling ball
waiting to see if it'll knock down one bowling pin or all ten.
Family and life are two things
Family, life, and happiness is one thing.
Life is a story for you to tell to the world.

Graphite Paradise
by Lauren Lee

A pencil hits a sheet of paper
it's a beautiful black and white scene,
where a paradise comes to life
full of pets, people, and trees.
In the very top right corner
the shining sun peeks through
a collection of cotton ball clouds
in a sky of the most perfect blue.
A beautiful bounty of butterflies
strolling through the air,
watches all the people taking pictures everywhere.
On my dining table, a drawing is complete,
but there's the tiniest hole in the corner
where a pencil hit the sheet of paper.

Nature's World
by Grace Finan

The prairie is dry and hot.
My eyes burn and water as the gray smoke rises.
The orange tongues of flame flicker,
eager to lick at anything in their path.
Thick humidity, and the strong scent of rich soil and dew,
are what fill the secluded garden.
I let the warm earth in my hand sift through my fingers.
The breeze rustles through the reeds on the dune.
It forces the sand to fly up in small whirlwinds.
It makes my shirt billow out behind me.
I can feel my hair streaming, as I run across the beach.
As the creek trickles, the brook babbles,
and the ocean crashes down on the sand,
I'll be in my yard, spinning,
as the rain pitter-patters all around me.

Lost In Darkness
by Tasnia Chowdhury

I'm lost
Nowhere to go
Nowhere to run
I'm trapped in
Obscurity
God kept me lost
with only my heart
My life could be gone,
I'm a person whose life
can be gone easily,
but only if God chooses,
until now I'll try
to see through my heart

It's Called Life
by Karina Rasner

I walk on an unknown path called life.
I don't know where it leads.
I don't know what I want,
I don't know what I need.
This confusing time is full of lies,
When I wonder what I should do.
I don't know if I should keep the old,
Or start up with the new.
What's right?
What's wrong?
So here is this song,
As unhelpful as it is.

I Believe
by Noah Gindele

I believe that everyone can change the world
I believe that you should be grateful about what you have
and not gripe about what you don't
I believe you should be kind even if people are not kind to you
I believe that people should try their best and never give up
I believe that families can fight
I believe people should always be them
I believe that it is wrong for people to take what is not theirs
I believe that the Golden Rule is the most important rule
I believe …

The Light That Went Away
by Jazlynn Barrera

Our life was bright
Like a light
It went dim
Because you left
And now it just flickers

Try
by Denis Melara

They say what would you do if you had flight?
But you don't need wings to fly.
What would you do if you had gills?
But you don't need gills to dive?
If you had super speed, where would you go?
But we've been to the moon and back, ya know.
So if you want to attempt the impossible,
Don't be afraid, just try.

A Life With Spice
by Colleen Schaner

All I really need to know, I learned in kindergarten.
All I really need to know about
how to live the spiciest life in town, I learned in kindergarten.
Wisdom was not $1,000,000, merely a dream,
but on the playground on the swing set. These are the things I learned:
Be humble when you really want to show everybody
something impressive that you did.
Use integrity, no matter how badly you want to blurt something out.
DO NOT force your poop out. (That's an important one.)
Don't eat too many marshmallows.
Life moves on.
Don't lose the class pet/stuffed animal, or drop it in the mulch.
Be a good sport, be happy for others--even if they surpass you a bit.
Don't drink rotten milk, or else you'll projectile vomit everywhere.
Don't jump in a puddle that clearly has a wet floor sign on it
in a hotel lobby, which will end up with you cracking your head open.
A very great lesson that I have learned, which is the key to life,
especially a spicy one, is to trust in God even in the darkest times.
You gotta have faith, 'cause that's the only way
you'll get through things like that, up and out of the ditch.
YOU CAN NEVER GIVE UP.
Everything you need to know is in there somewhere.

I Tried
by Tessa Holt

I felt you slip past me
You didn't stop
I watched you
for an hour
You didn't wave
I helped you
when no one else would
You didn't smile
I waited awhile
slowly losing hope
You didn't come

Apple Cores and Sly Foxes
by Margaret McMullin

Why is it that I forget about how amazing humans are?
Maybe because some aren't.
Some are rotten like a week old apple core, hollow and bitter.
Some are like foxes, elegant from afar
but as soon as you take a step toward them they will hiss and run away.
Or maybe it's because I've had many foul experiences
with foxes and week old apple cores.
Yet I have met some extraordinary people.
People who will take you under their wing and love you.
People who will make you feel giddy
and make you laugh your lungs out when you're around them.
But sometimes these extraordinary people turn into foxes
and week old apple cores, and take you by surprise.
When they nurture you it suddenly feels like they are doing it out of pity
and love seems like charity work.
When you laugh with them it seems as though
now they are laughing at you.
I guess in the end it's harder to determine if an apple core is really rotten
or you left it out too long.
I guess in the end it's harder to tell if the fox is here to stay
or will scamper away at your first step.
I guess humans are amazing.
Amazing at tricking you.
Amazing at loving you.
Yes, amazing.

Snow
by Mary Moore

It's a still night.
There's not a sound.
There is white
All around.
It's falling down
One by one.
When it's done,
It's so much fun.
When it's winter
It sometimes falls.
You need a coat
And maybe some gloves.
You can play in it
All day.
Until the sun
Melts it away.

Smoke
by Owen Thornton

We are stiffened as we watch our enemy blow,
Shook by the wind, dancing to and fro.
Our enemy is the gray smoke,
The killing smog that will make you choke.
This was all caused by greed,
A message, but did they heed?
Of course not, why would they?
"Someone else will give it up," they thought that early morning in May.
And the want for those vehicles led to this,
A gray world filled with deathly steam in every cave and crevice.
Then it condensed and fell as acid, burning,
It ruined buildings and water, churning.
We had all lost any remaining scraps of hope,
But they created a project that would stop our mope.
They made a humongous white rocket,
That would fly around the world and stuff the smoke into its pocket.
And then it would change course,
Go far out into space and explode, no remorse.
We all gathered for the launch at the one uninfected lake,
Hoping that right now, after all this, that its promise wouldn't break.
It lifted, it blew, and as we looked up the sky started to clear!
I smiled, for the time was near.

Why She Is My Best Friend
by Paige Gerads

She is my best friend in the world
for several reasons
She doesn't care what I look like
Or how I do in school
She just cares about who I am
The person I am when I am around her
She's my friend because
She makes me laugh
She brings out the best in me
I bring out the best in her
I make her laugh
Like we saw once
God made us best friends
Because He knew our parents couldn't handle us as sisters.
Because we were made to be
Best friends forever
Inseparable

The Color, the Flower, and My Best Friend
by Samantha Ryder

There is one person that inspires me
And her name starts with a V
She is a color and a flower
She helps me every day, every hour
Her name is a dark purple or a blue
It's a pretty color, yes that's true
Her personality is like a petal, soft and caring
And not like metal, sharp and daring
Has anyone guessed what her name is yet
Well I'll tell you
It's Violet
Violet is one of my best friends
I hope she stays like that
Till the end
I have many more best friends, too
But Violet and my friendship is true!

Football Dream
by Ethan Wiens

I would be the sophisticated OBJ
Or the cutting-edge Bo Jackson
The king of the game that nobody's passin'
I would be the star of the team
And the star of the league
And everybody would be calling
From Channel 53
I would have people lined up
All the way up and down street, Sea 936 blocking the view
The smell is overpowering
And the noise is deafening and it's almost in my grip
But ...
everybody knows
that this is
Just a dream

A Friend
by Anna Freeman

Blessing, Blessing, oh Blessing
Chirping happily
Blue as the waves on the beach
Laughing joyously
Pretty as the morning sky
Pretty, pretty parakeet
Blessing, Blessing, oh Blessing
Singing a glad song
Beautiful and wonderful
Always curious
Never was a truer song
Pretty, pretty parakeet
Blessing, Blessing, oh Blessing
Chirping and singing
Prettier than a flower
You are a true friend
A friend like you who can find?
Pretty, pretty parakeet

Life
by Regan O'Neill

A gift for many,
A burden for some,
An intricate gift,
Of only one.
A series of journeys,
Leading to one path.
The one thing that binds
Us to our pasts,
Is the love that
Will always last.

Where's Daddy?
by Tom Weon

I woke up in the car, because I heard someone softly crying.
It's Mommy. I ask, "Mommy, why are you crying? Where are we going?"
"To the hospital," she smiles back.
But. The smile feels fake, forced, and sad.
"Where's Daddy?"
"We'll see him soon," Mommy said, and I keep quiet for the rest of the ride.
When we get to the hospital, Mommy puts me in a room to wait.
Outside, I can hear shouting and people arguing.
I can sort of hear Mommy's voice through all the voices.
Something about surgery and critical condition.
Whatever that means.
Mommy and a man with some red paint on his mint colored shirt
argue about some adult things.
Then the entire room goes silent
as our ears are stuffed with a long annoying beep.
It doesn't stop. It doesn't stop. Just keeps going and going.
It's annoying.
I wish it would stop.
After I get used to it, I can hear someone crying their heart out.
Then Mommy comes back in.
I think she was the one crying really hard.
I decide to ask her one more time.
"Where's Daddy?"
"In a better place now."

Darkness
by Josh Kempe

I flood the barren room in an icy black ink,
And as you slowly breathe in and out,
I course vigorously through your body,
Making your blood run cold,
Then boiling it with the crimson flames of anger and resent,
And as I roar through your mind, I engulf every happy memory,
Turning its sweet and golden rays of light into bitterness and regret,
Until you are hollowed,
Nothing more than a suit I wear,
And as your eyelids close for the last time,
I am all you see,
All you fear,
All you are.
But even in the most darkest of night,
There are some brave enough to turn on the light.

Fear
by Isabella Rodriguez

I am the shivering, shaking worry,
The cold that eats you at night
The black crow that caws
The harsh winter jaws
The thing that won't let you take flight
I seize up your courage
Your bravery
Your life
In your mind I can make a flower a knife
I'm more powerful than anything in your imagination
To summon me doesn't take much concentration
But in the end
I keep you alive
I'll make you run so you can survive
No need to worry
I'll always be here
Right by your side
Your old friend, Fear

Pig
by Solveig Fellows

There once was a pig named Hubert
He liked to listen to Mozart and Schubert
He was pale pink
His feet did stink
And he liked to eat vanilla yogurt

I Am From
by Beesan ElKhatib

I am from pita bread dipped in oil then coated with a delicious spice blend.
I am from meat layered with tomato and lettuce hugged by a toasty bun,
Oh, and you can't forget about the ketchup and mustard!
I am from staying up till morning and my friends in America being confused
Why the time says 0:15 on my Snapchat story.
I am from wondering why my country
Decided to use the numbers 1-12 two times a day.
And as a little kid trying to figure out if it was 12:15 AM or PM
I am from long beautiful dresses
Embroidered with intricate flowers and colorful swirls
I am from indigo ripped jeans, and a superhero T-shirt
Paired with black Converse.
I am from group dances, with unique kicks and jumps
Paired with upbeat and audience pumping music
I am from the latest dance move from the latest cool artist
Seeming like an endless trend, but dying out with time.
I am from stretchy sugary candy
That comes in many different shapes and flavors.
From strawberry tasting teeth to Coca Cola bottles
I am from candy for all your different moods
Dum Dum? Or Smarties? They have it all for you here
I am from a cursive-styled language
Where all the letters are connected to one another in a word
A language that goes from right to left. A beauty, containing 28 letters.
An art, with no distinction between uppercase and lowercase.
An allure that makes you want to dance when you speak it
I am from a language in which every letter is independent
A language that goes from left to right. A beauty, containing 26 letters.
An art with uppercase and lowercase variations of every letter.
An allure that makes you want to talk forever.
I am from two countries, two cultures, two people,
Palestine and America, blended together to make me, me.
I bleed black, green, white, and red.
But at the same time, I bleed red, white, and blue.

A Flower
by Clara Buchner

The world is a marvel of nature
Venturing out into space
So strong it seems you can't break it
With pain or with man or machine
But the world is only a flower
A blossom trying its luck
It is strong compared to a dewdrop
It is nothing compared to a rock
And what on Earth am I thinking
If I should dare to defy
The monster that hides in the closet
The thing we have come to call time
You can look straight at it and miss it
The ever present fact of it all
Because the world is here all around us
And the clocks just hang in the wall
Forever is never forever
For those of us living on Earth
This world is only a flower
Brief color that springs from the dirt

Dreams
by Alleathea Pfeifer

Dreams live in your heart
Shine in the night
Prove to the light
To be true
Dreams are wishes
That you hope to come true
Life is full of dreams
Dreams are full of life
People dream of wonderful things
Wonderful things are what life brings
Dreams will come true
If you keep on dreaming
Dreams, dreams, dreams
Dreams are treasures
We hold close to our hearts
We dream and dream
And dream some more
Until morning comes
Then we hold them dear
Keep on dreaming

Lies
by Natalie Pineda-Salas

There once was a girl who lied
She lied about everything
She lied about being fine
You didn't hear what she really said
now she is greeting death
she wore that same smile
You were so fooled
she held up the tool
oh the lies she told
she is ready to go
leave everything behind
All she leaves are lies

My Room
by Jordan Kipp

The shimmering gray walls sing a slow lullaby.
But the clutter screams like the world is falling apart.
The window is wide open
And the summer breeze comes flooding in.
The sweet scent of tulips
And swaying trees engulfs it.
Soft stuffed animals line the walls,
Like soldiers guarding the queen's castle.
Books are scattered
Waiting to be caught by the worn hands
Of someone who wants to share in their story.

Wolves
by Ornina Yousef

I wait in the shadows that creep through the night,
My heart roughly pounding to bound and to bite.
My pack stands beside me, not back or in front.
We sit in the darkness and wait for the hunt.
The deer lifts its head, we hold back our growls.
Then moonlight comes rushing and all the pack howls.
We quickly surround the poor helpless deer.
It looks for an exit but nothing is near.
With one killing bite, we capture its life,
Faster than the slash of the sharpest knife.
We feast in great pleasure beneath mother moon,
And know that our time will come again soon.

I Roam In Your Mind
by Mitchell Forrest

I'm dark and threatening to other people
When you let me, I take over your body
I won't stop until you get what you want
Sadness, happiness, the world
When I take you over you get really hot
You turn bright red in fact
My weakness is happiness
Those friends of yours abolish my control over you
I cloud your mind like a wisp of smoke
Unable to think
I turn you into a raging beast

Fall's Last Sunset
by Eric Blaine

I was walking through the forest to see it before the first snow.
I waited to admire the nature and its mysterious ways.
I could hear a river in the distance with a squirrel near searching for nuts.
I watched as he touched each thing he could find for food to fatten up.
As the sun set I could see a glow off the water and leaves.
As I went further I could smell the earth and leaves all around me.
As I was engulfed by the beauty of it all,
I watched the sun set for that was the end of fall.

Where I'm From
by Seyi Benson

I'm from the hot sunny summer days
Slick with sweat in the valley.
From sweet yummy
Chilled ice cream for the hot summer day.
I'm from the summer's hot damp air,
The sweat sticks to my clothes.
I'm from running, cool rushes of air
Whip past me and into the warm night air.
I'm from beautiful family photos
that I could spend hours looking at
and getting lost in them.
I'm from some family sewn dresses,
That shine in the light.
I'm from, "We love because He first loved us" (1 John 4:19).
I'm from deliciously homemade fried rice
that makes me want more and more.
I'm from caring for babies and holding them close.

Challenge
by Brandy Smith

I hear this all the time.
You can't do it, you're too weak
Well almost every time they say that
I do the 'impossible'
If it was impossible, I can't do it,
And I did.
Do yourself a favor,
Don't challenge me.

Waiting
by Aria Beaulieu-Flolo

You sit and wait for nothing.
It's like grasping your hands into thin air.
Waiting for world problems to be solved,
Waiting for hunger, poverty to all end.
But your hands remain vacant
Or on a smaller note
Waiting outside in the cold
For someone you don't know at all.
Or waiting for that bully to stop
Pinching, punching, or pushing
If you're old enough to realize what I'm saying
You're old enough to help me make a change
So together we can change the world
Love is in our grasp.

My Vivid Vision
by Christian Johnson

My vision is a close-up side focus of a yellow Monarch butterfly.
The outline of the butterfly's wings are black with white spots.
The black outside of his delicate wings
Spread magnificently through them like veins on a leaf.
He is standing boldly on the bumpy lime green pollen
in the center of the dazzling yellow flower.
The flower's petals are as droopy as a flag on a day with no wind
And they shine like golden ingots as the sun reflects off of them.
In the background there is the unclear picture
of more yellow flowers shimmering in the light.
It's quite the sight and my hope is you see my vision as well,
Maybe in such a way where it is even better and 10 times more swell.
The rest is just a blur, you can't even tell.

Tennis
by Kaylee Prins

Early morning, sunny day
grab your racket, it's time to play
hit the ball over the net
play with friends you just met
back and forth flies the ball
point, the referee will call
Game over now

Moving On
by Dylan Urvig

Deep in the dark night, cloudless and clear
he followed the illuminated trail
where dense grass surrounds
Nothing to take or lose, he forged on
He had left his life and hand in the cold damp sand
He had to move faster
run from it all, leave everything behind
Nothing to lose
No family, no friends
he moved on
No home, no food
Travel is done
All of it in the damp sand burning
Nowhere to go, nowhere to run
everything lost

The Gardener
by Olivia Brockman

She tends to the flowers,
her weathered hands never tire.
Day and night,
she extracts beauty from only her fingertips,
while beads of perspiration form on her brow.
Her favorites are the roses,
dyed red from the blood of her exhaustion,
glistening with the drops of morning dew.
She feeds them with her love,
her callused fingers caressing their emerald leaves,
the sunflowers shading her steady back.
Only when the garden withers,
and diamonds fall from the clouds,
will she lay among the frosted rosebush,
and rest.

The Flash Before My Eyes
by Brooke Grewe

I wake up and see the sky
I see this bird take off and fly
The sky is bright
Nobody in sight
I go downstairs
But I see the flares
The sun is bright
But full of might
I close my eyes
I open them back up
To see
My family
So sad
I go and ask
To hear my mom say
I'm sorry but your grandma died
I burst into tears
And think of all my fears

The Kits
by Leah Johnson

Pitter patter little kitten feet
Tiny little mewls calling for mommy
The litter is hungry
Padding slowly, trying to make the time last before kits attack
Climbing trees and digging holes
The kits play all day
Time for a catnap! Soon they are up and running
Mom is sleeping and the kits leap
Soon it's time to eat
The kits ignore their mother's call
Soon here comes mom
Soon a leader calls to cats
Here are kits six months old
The little ones are jealous
They wait to be apprenticed
The new apprentices reassure
The kits shall have mentors
They will be great apprentices

Truth
by Faaya Adem

You call us names that should never be spoken,
Do things that should never be done.
You tear us down,
Throw us to the ground.
Only to stand right back up,
As we don't fear the power you hold over us.
We know we might not be able to change the world,
But we will never stop trying.
People will insult us,
Hurt us,
Do everything they can to upset us.
And you know what?
Just because we are crying doesn't mean you have broken us,
It just means that we have a heart that can be broken.
You are nothing without us,
And we are everything without you.
Your hatred shows us that we are equal,
That we are strong and that all we need is love.

The Revolutionary War
by Andie Hirz

Freedom is what we seek, freedom is what we fight for
Our cold bare feet on the snow, but freedom is what we see in our future
BOOM! BOOM!
Blood then death, another man down
I must keep going, I must keep fighting
I must earn my freedom, our county's freedom
Days, weeks, months pass
The days grow warmer, hot, heat
What's that I hear?
July 4th, 1776, we've signed the Declaration of Independence!
But the war goes on as the days get colder and hotter
Cold hot, cold hot
The years go on
It's death for others, but not for me as we push on as army together
Finally the day comes!
September 3rd, 1783, we are free from the war!
It's over and I am safe and alive
But most importantly we are a free country
And they call us
The United States of America

You Don't
by Aiden Blaeser

You don't even know what I go through,
Who I am, what I do.
Why try, why work for it
When you're just going to say no.
You purposely hurt me
Then you say are you okay,
Like nothing happened
I'm done, if you do that you need to STOP.
Why do you do it.
Ask yourself, why? Why? Why?
Why am I doing this?
If you're hurt, why hurt others
Do you want people to be miserable like you
Because that's what you're doing.
Don't take it out on others,
Go to a counselor, friend, someone you can trust.
It's not fun, I know that because I've experienced it.
It's hard but those people can help
I thought I would just keep it to myself
But after I went through it, I knew I should've
I ask myself, why? Why? Why didn't I.

I Am
by Samantha May

I am courageous and silly.
I wonder what my mom is doing right now.
I hear my hamster still scurrying around.
I see my hamster playing around.
I want to be an Olympic gymnast.
I am courageous and silly.
I feel very happy when I have downtime.
I worry about my sister.
I cry when my animals die.
I am courageous and silly.
I understand my teachers are very busy.
I say, "Oh my gosh," all the time.
I dream that every girl is treated the same as every boy.
I try to always keep my friends happy.
I hope that every person in the world will learn to be nice to one another.
I am courageous and silly.

Basketball
by Alexis Gilbertson

Tip off
Your team has the ball
You shoot
You hear the ball swish in the net
You make a 3
Can't make more
You get taken out of the game
You go back in
You shoot at the last second
It swishes
You win the game for the team
You fall to the floor
Your team is around you
You are so excited
You and your team are going
TO THE CHAMPIONSHIP GAME!

Hurry Up and Shoot Already!!!
by Jenna Corbett

The sweat dripping down my face. Legs so tired from running.
Time running out. Two minutes on the clock.
The pressure of the buzzer draining on the team.
The ball with the other team.
It's time one of my teammates whispers to me.
My teammate and I ambush the ball.
I get it, pass to a teammate.
She dribbles down the court. Passes to me.
I dribble it to the foul line.
I square up at the basket.
Four seconds left on the clock.
Time ticking away.
Here I am, all the weight and pressure of the clock all on me.
Got to make this shot I say to myself.
I shoot. It's heading toward the basket.
It hits the rim. Goes in circles.
It goes in right when the buzzer goes off.
I made it, I scream.
Everyone screams. "We did it, we won!!!"

On Top of the World
by Callie Valeri

Skip, skip,
Leap, leap
Prancing in a field of daisies,
I'm singing
And dancing
All around
I am having the time of my life
The sun is large and bright
And yet I am not bothered
Nothing could change how I am feeling
I am on top of the world
All of a sudden
I hear something
It is a faint buzzing
Bzzz ...
Bzzz ...
And then ...
I wake up
Oh well.

Muteboy
by Vivian Eldridge

Voice? What's that?
I don't have one of those, but hey,
It wasn't my choice.
Someone new in someplace old,
Lifting up spirits that are already soaring,
What about mine?
I can hardly lift my own.
Why not try someone else? But hey,
It's not my choice.
But then you talked to me even though I couldn't say anything back.
You could read me. Easier than any book.
You didn't laugh at me.
You laughed with me.
You invited me over. Stood up to me. Showed me something beautiful.
That was your choice.
I love you.
I love you.
I love you.
And that's my choice.

Our Flag
by Michelle Bae

Slash, slash, slash
While swords clash
Boom, boom, boom
And the bombs go boom
And all I do?
Sit and wait, standing here witnessing an important war
Will I stand tall?
Or will I fall?
Sewn for a cause?
Or become nothing at all
As dawn rises,
They all look up to see me
Battered, but still standing
Then a roar fills the air
Of men crying out
Screams of victory!

Smooth Sailing
by Maddie McCay

Well guys, I'll tell you,
Being your daughter is no smooth sailing,
There's been huge waves,
And nightmarish creatures,
And hurricanes too,
And sometimes the ship began to sink down,
But all this time, from one dad telling me
to stop taking pictures on his phone
and blowing deathly smoke rings in my stoic face,
To the other "old one", not even being a physical memory,
My mother and sister stay on watch, never veering course with me,
We have been learning to patch up the holes in the sails
and the leaks in the boat, and it's ok, because I know someday
we will reach that beautiful, orange mess in the sky
the sun makes at 6:45 on a summer's night.
So since we have made it this far, let's not turn back to the docks,
Because you will find it's hard to steer a ship in this world,
And before you know it, we will all be in that sunset,
But right now,
Being your daughter is no smooth sailing.

Life
by Tristen Wibbels

Life is a weird thing
but I like it
because it's amazing
It's cool how we smell,
how living things are creative,
how we taste,
and can't forget
the best thing in the world.
us.

My Dog
by Kaili Wheeler

My dog is very dumb
I am very smart
He sits on the toilet
Reading *Moby Dick*
He does my homework
Cleans my room
Makes my bed
Wait a minute
What did you say
He is the smart one
Not a chance

A Dream
by Priya Kommu

Dreams are spotlights egging you on
Yet at some points slowing you down
You feel you need to shine brighter
But in dark times they are your only source of light
Dreams are hugs enveloping you in greatness and love
But can be suffocating when trying to fulfill
Dreams are a box, keeping you inside
But at the same time, forcing you to think outside the box
Dreams are an old pair of jeans, fitting your every needs
you know their every seam and tear
know soon they'll have to retire but always be there

Gymnastics
by Brenna Thordson

Great
Yearly
MAGA gymnastics
Neat
Awesome
Super fun
Teamwork
Is hard
Cool
Summer

Home At Last
by Sarah Donnelly

Some kids wait in orphanages reading a story
and dream of living with a family in all the glory.
Children wait in orphanages for years
and think of their future families trying to hold back tears.
A man and woman come by and see me,
then they come in to fill out paperwork as I sit there with glee.
I love my mom and dad with all my heart,
my thanks to them for a brand new start.
Don't know much about my past,
but I do know I'm home at last.

Blue Shoes
by Molly Leners

I have a home,
But I don't live alone.
I have all of my memories of my family,
just wait and you will see.
It was 1932 when I had my little girl,
I was screaming, I am going to hurl.
My husband left me for my friend,
this is not when my misery would end.
I bought my baby nice little shoes,
They were a light happy sky blue.
She got sick and said achoo!
That is when I said, don't leave me here, I love you.
She came back as an angel and said,
I will never leave you here alone,
For you are my mom and for this is my home.

The Truth
by LaKeysha Larson

I can see you but you don't see me.
I'm talking but you're not listening
I wish that you'd see me more than just a little girl, but a young adult.
I wish you'd see more than just my flaws or the shape of my body.
There is more in a person than their looks or body size.
See people for who they are and not for what you wanna see.

Sometimes I Go ...
by Madelyn Thomson

Sometimes I go to give my hand a lend,
sometimes I go to stretch and bend.
Sometimes I go down a street I don't know,
where my biggest schoolmates are giant tall foes.
Sometimes I go to a tree, and when I go there, I can feel free.
Sometimes I go to a river that never ends,
or maybe I go to somewhere where it never descends.
Sometimes I go somewhere to go and weep,
sometimes I go somewhere where there are secrets I keep.

The Last Kind of Power
by Caitlin Boman

Oceans, oceans breath takes our soul,
Like fire in our eyes
Also so like power in someone's hands
Hands, hands to move,
move to move, moment to moment
Life on line, on the edge.
Like a wire,
Someone walking on wire,
Building on life and life
You don't know what to say or do when you're on the line ...
Pondering ... is like where you try and save the environment ...
Where you're gonna be free and wild
Like a wolf and hunt down animals and survive
Survive is like you try and hold on to breath
Breath is like to go and find your own passion
Passion is like ponder,
curiosity is like a cat trying to figure out a puzzle under 5 seconds
5 seconds is like a timer under 1 second.
Trying to escape, like on the escape button
Trying to get out of the game, but you're not controlled but you are
It doesn't get it?

Baseball
by Damon Thoemke

I hit the ball
Crack!
It's soaring in the air over the fence.
I'm at shortstop waiting for the pitch
My glove is so clean it makes all the girls scream.
When I pitch it looks like slow motion to me
But to the batter it looks like the ball is a bullet train.
My curve is so good I have all these batters
S
  h
    o
      o
        k
It starts right at them, and then breaks their knees.
I'll school you in baseball, to challenge me you have to be a fool
I know you think you're cool,
but c'mon, if you really wanna get on my level you need a step stool.

Divorce Dog
by Rowan Johns

The school day is done and I'm thinking of Jake,
as I ride home to see my best friend
With his velvet-like ears and his super-sad eyes,
he runs round and round with no end
Cuddles and treats, we're no longer apart
My day has been full, but now so is my heart
Loud wheels squeal and I'm off to the gate, will he step off that yellow bus?
He's there! He's there! I'm barking with glee. It's now just the two of us
Cuddles and treats, kisses and play
It's late afternoon, but the start of my day
The school day is done and I'm thinking of Jake,
I wonder what he's doing this minute
I don't see him today so I know he's upset.
We both love each other with no limit
Sighs and tears, as I miss my best friend
My day has been full, but it's sad at the end
Loud wheels squeal and I'm off to the gate. Nobody steps off the bus
My buddy's not here and it's breaking my heart.
There's no one to make all the fuss
Sighs and tears as I whine away
It's late afternoon, but the end of my day

3rd Place

Ella Sran

I Define Myself
by Ella Sran

I will not be defined by stereotypes
I am not a living accessory that belongs in the kitchen
Nor the clearer of your mess
I was not made for your pleasure
Nor does my value derive from my looks
I can run just as fast, punch just as hard, work just as much
My sisters and I will go through so much more
than many will ever know
Before you call us weak, master our challenges
And then tell me what you think
Do not stray to the mindset where women hang on a cliff of weakness
Where only men can lift them up
We can pull ourselves up
As we have for centuries
Do not think of me as a doll or a fool
I am strong, fierce and raw
I will not be defined by stereotypes
I define myself

2nd Place

Nicole Patrock

Cardboard Castles
by Nicole Patrock

As I passed by this old box
wedged between two dumpsters,
it reminded me
of the forts and castles
I had created as a child
from cartons just like that.
Once inside, I would curl up
and often fall asleep
feeling safe and protected
within my cardboard womb.
But this box at my feet,
discarded and unwanted,
was the only home
for the woman inside.
She lay awake, unblinking,
clutching her knees to her chest,
scared, alone, and crying
within her cardboard tomb.
As a child she, too, had
played in castles and forts.

1st Place

Hailey Cheon

Hailey's work was submitted to us
while she was a student in the seventh grade.
With a flair for descriptive writing,
we can see why she excels in the literary arts.
Congratulations, Hailey!

Gluttony
by Hailey Cheon

when i was little i sipped my mother's words
like tea on a summer's afternoon,
it danced on my tongue and
from my lips sprang new words,
they came out sweet like cold lemonade
and sang a song of peace and innocence.
when i grew they accused me of gluttony
as they shoved words down my throat
and i was taught to swallow.
they say that america is a place of free speech,
but they forgot to mention that
you cannot speak when your voice is stuffed
with words that are not your own.
the next time that they put a knife up to my throat
and tell me to swallow,
i will let them cut
because then at least
my throat can sing a song
that it has been dying to sing
ever since you muted me

Division III

Grades 8-9

Beach
by Mackenzie McCracken

I run towards the crashing waves.
Dive into the water and swim around.
The sun's rays are as hot as a roaring fire.
The fish swimming below me tickle my feet.
Feel the sand in between my toes.
Build sandcastles in the sand.
Take long walks where water meets sand.
Smell the salty air around me.
Fly a kite in the cool breeze.
Crash!!
Hear the waves crash onto the sand.
Little crabs run across the sand,
To their sand holes in the ground for safety.
Watch the birds fly above.
Lay on the sand and relax,
And tan until I get a sunburn.
Watch the sunset on the horizon.
Fall asleep after a tiring day.
I love the beach.

My Dearest
by Brody Janssen

This poem is for the one and the one only, my dearest love.
When you smile it feels like the warm summer's rays are shining on me.
When you look at me I stop in amazement and ponder off into outer space.
When you feel down it feels like I got hit by a brick in the back
or pricked by a needle.
When my eyes meet your eyes my eyes blush and want to cry in the beautifulness.
When I am in the same room it feels like the whole class isn't even there anymore.
When we sit by each other it's like we're touching
and it feels like a soft pillow is right by me.
When we talk it sounds like an angel is talking to me.
When we give each other gifts it's like God is giving me a gift.
When we meet each other it's like God gave me my own angel right by me.
Then when we get old it will still feel the same
but we will be in the same room all the time.
And when you die it will be like I have no light on me anymore.
And when you die I will never feel like I do now.
And when I die I will be with you again.
When we live in Heaven it will just be the same as we were when we were alive.

Black History Month
by Nya Lloyd

People.
We are all different.
From the way we look,
To the color of our skin,
And from the culture we are inherited in.
We are put in these positions because of who we are.
Martin Luther King made a difference by far.
Many others have stood up for us.
For citizenship and the pursuit of happiness.
A month was created for a reason yet to be.
Now I fully understand why we have Black History.
People.
We are all still different,
Still from the way we look,
Still from the color of our skin,
And still from the culture we are inherited in.

Hope
by Marisa Del Borrello

I listen
As the river makes its way down
the mountain of hope.
hope that I counted on.
hope that I needed.
There is only the sound of when river meets rock
Birds whistling in the wind
as I stand and watch
the river seems to go slower
as it makes its way down
this mountain that I created.
it seems like I wait there forever
like a moment in time
that never continues,
then it dawns on me,
like something snapping inside of me
that hope is a game,
that shouldn't be played.

My Life
by Elaine Danielsen

When I was born
The world gained a weirdo
That weirdo had a dark past
from when she was little
She pretends that it never happened
But her depression seeps through to the surface
She is afraid it will happen again
When in school she acts fine
But anyone knows otherwise
She never cares
And that's fine

Dear Mom
by Daniel Avalos Lara

When the first moment when I saw light
You were there
When the moments when I played in the park
or hold my hand to cross the street
You were there
I loved you with all my heart, you were my life
I could never live without you
But when I got older things got rough
I treated you bad, I disrespected you
I never gave you a kiss on the cheek in middle school
because I thought only of my friends
I never thought to give you anything for Mother's Day,
I only gave you a hug
But now that you are gone
I wish I could go back and kiss you when I was in middle school
I wish I had given you some chocolate when it was Mother's Day
I wish I had you back again
but now I am there alone standing in your grave
Each year when it was your birthday or when it was Mother's Day
I gave you a gift
I left it in your grave
The only thing I heard when she died was ... I love you
I never said anything when she said that
but when I was in her grave I started to cry
I love you too, Mom, thank you for this life that you have gave me
Respect and love your mom
also take time to know her before the time runs out

You Can't Break a Broken Heart
by Mikaylah Saunders

The sunset passed,
February 17, 2017
The dark sad trees
I watched you turn your back and leave
I hate you 'cause you make me cry
When all you ever do is lie
Yet I still wish that you were mine
But I like to tell myself, "I'm fine"
It feels like I've been ripped apart
But you can't break a broken heart
Everyone tells me that it's okay
But I need you every single day
It kills me that I know you lied
And still, you're perfectly fine
I hope that life treats you good
Don't worry about me, I didn't think you would
So this is goodbye I guess, we'll still be friends
But I will love you till the end

The Want
by Katie McGushin

Want is a verb
The meaning, to desire
Is that what you can call this feeling?
To simply hope for, to fancy?
Is this how this feeling is described?
The burning inside that cannot be simply placed
I can't put a name to what I want
I just want for something more
More than what is being given
It's not materialistic
Not really a hope or a dream
Just a burning
Need is a verb
Its meaning, to require for essentially
Do I need whatever this is?
Do I need it to survive?
It feels like I might
But I know I don't
Why is it that I need for something more?

Beyond Beliefs
by Laura Dunkleberger

They loom and they creak
as if they wanted to meet
They speak of lands
where they can't even stand
They fall upon a spell
which they can't tell
They capture animals
like a bunch of cannibals
They die
as the seasons go by
The trees kept it inside
as their leaves turned dry
The trees
The trees

Just a Book
by Emily Koberlein

A book is not just two covers with a couple hundred pages in between,
it's so much more than that.
You walk into a book, you find yourself wandering through the pages,
exploring each and every word,
as if it were a glistening present on Christmas morning.
You skip through the chapters, leaping from page to page,
anxiously awaiting what will happen next, and you begin to question
a million different things in your head, all at once.
A book is an escape, a treasure, a map, an adventure.
A book is something that gives you the opportunity to express emotion
and thoughts just by reading, by reading you're filling your mind
with knowledge of the unknown, the questioned, and the mysterious.
allowing yourself to find new things behind every word.
A book offers a new place, a place where you can let your mind be free
of the worrisome, troubled world,
where you can find yourself by reading about others.
Escaping into a book allows you to view your own situations
through another person's eyes.
It allows you to explore your options by watching the characters
take chances, risks you could never take yourself.
There are so many things I've learned from books,
that talking to a million people, or nobody at all, could have ever taught me.
Reading has helped me find my own words, my voice,
and a passion I never knew I possessed.
A book is something that helps you discover how strong your mind can be,
and how inspiring and beautiful others' words can be.
It never has been and never will be, "just a book," to me.

My Heaven
by Jackson Ely

It starts with growing up there,
I lived at the beach from when I was born till 3 years old.
I have never gotten over that day when we moved:
It was the saddest day of my life.
I always hoped I could stay there forever.
I now look forward to every Thanksgiving,
when we head back down there for a week.
The water is as clear as glass
and the same temperature in June and November.
The views are pictures you used to only dream of
It feels like I should be there every day
and I should have to be called in for dinner
It has food you can only dream of till you have it.
It has everything I would want in a place:
Sports, family, food, and fun, and it's surrounded by water.
You wake up to the salty smell of the ocean,
and go to sleep hearing the quiet sounds of animals.
In my mind it should be the definition of paradise,
I don't think there is a greater place on Earth.
You may argue that your paradise is better,
but I think mine can never be surpassed

Silently Speaking
by Justin Bonny

A bright light surrounds me.
I am asleep in the hospital bed
A breathing tube is in place
Restraints around my arms
I can't speak
I try to utter words but sound won't come out
I try screaming but nothing will work
A warm blanket covers me and I fall asleep
Seconds later I snap awake, I try to breathe on my own
But my lungs won't work
The ventilator breathes for me
I try to fight back
It feels like a war between me and the machine
I try breathing once more
After several minutes of nothing I finally work up enough strength to breathe
Weak at first but then it becomes strong
I can't hear my thoughts, only machines
If feels as though the constant beeping of machines have taken over my life
Soon I will be free from these machines but for now all I can do is wait.

Partner In Crime
by Isabelle Gracias

Partner in crime is a person who holds the key to your heart.
We run down the roads laughing at our victim who we scared to death.
Never stopping, never regretting.
We are a shadow in the night that can't be caught
until the sun shows our shadows.
Slowly we are separated by the dreadful school
who holds us hostage for 8 hours.
When released we come up with a plan for our next crime and new victim.
I am the strong one, you are stealthy, I rob a bank, you bring the car,
I hotwire a car, you buckle us up, for then we don't die.
Being a partner in crime means that we take bullets for each other
but most importantly we would do anything for each other.
Our days are done, as we get separated by your move.
I cry every day, hiding behind a mask of fake happiness.

Dreamworld
by Sophie Dattilo

You are useless.
You can make slideshows, you can write speeches,
but nothing will fill the hole of your middle-aged ignorance.
You can scare children for an hour, but an hour later, the mark is gone,
the cushioned blow you delivered is irrelevant.
They will resort back to the ways they were scared out of,
back to the ways pressure has branded into their minds.
And now your blind eye sees the clearest,
delivering nothing of what you will include in your next speech.
Infinity continues.
Because to get your message across you need power behind your words,
But powerful words are never heard by ears that don't want to listen.
The delicacy of your ecosystem will be your downfall one day,
Because there are no doubts in logical minds that your façade will fail.
But how does a façade fail if you don't know it's there?
So I am dearly sorry to say that your attempts are futile,
although humorous to those cynical enough to laugh.
You will never imprint their minds,
no matter how hard you force authority down their throats.
No, it will float from their bowels and drift right into oblivion,
where the rest of your attempts reside.
You have never experienced.
You lived in a world of kindness,
but the world is a lot harsher for the children of today.
Time has taken a cruel turn.
Wake up.
This is me shattering the glass of your dreamworld.

Broken
by Katelynn Shea

Something's not right
In your eyes there's no light
Something's not there
But where, but where?
I can see it in your eyes
What you're feeding me is lies
You're not okay, but you won't tell
I know you hide a pain you can't quell
Eyes are the window to the soul
And you're there stuck in a hole
Your window is shattering
And everything's clattering
To the ground it all falls
And echoes through the halls
All I want to do is fix it, and I try
But I lose myself in the process, while you fly
Something's not right, and I can't find the key
But I look inside, and what's broken is me.

A Siren's Song
by Victoria Forsyth

A song, sweet and calm,
a tale about a sailor's fall
there is no help around, no island with a single palm
three enchanting girls floated on top of the water, they are ever so tall
Their dresses made of water that sparkle all day
the men and women on the ship jumping off
no one knows if Sirens are fey,
the men and women's minds invaded as they die off
The three girls' hair billowing in the breeze,
while their eyes reflect a sunrise
the sight of them would make any man freeze
they only sang but their song was one of the wise
As the last man sank,
the girls danced away
the people all drowned because of how much water they drank
everyone wished the Sirens didn't stay
There wasn't even time for screams,
the water turned red
The men and women now only exist in dreams
while the rest of the world lay unaware in their bed
When the girls left, it was with such stealth
as they went to take away another boat's health

What Comes Next?
by Grace Campiti

What comes next?
Only fate will know
Will I be successful once I grow?
Or will I tumble like a weed,
Once I'm freed
Without a way to go?
What comes next?
This is my time
To choose the path that's rightfully mine.
I am a branch with many leaves.
Ready to choose my way with ease.
It's time to begin the climb.

Unknown Fear
by Paige Carver

We're all just trying to make it out on the other side alive.
But we fear we'll break before then.
Fear we won't make it because we aren't as strong as the others.
Fear that something insanely tragic will happen that we can't handle.
And we'll simply break down.
Fall apart in front of everyone.
Because we can't control when it happens.
Or how it happens.
It's all just a mystery.

My Journey
by Vanessa Perez

My journey at school was like a mountain I had to scale
Almost every year, at some point, I thought I would fail
I sometimes felt pain, I sometimes felt breathless excitement
Most days school was fun, but sometimes it was like confinement
As time went by, I learned to appreciate school and my teachers
My friends and my learning experience, all of their features
School taught me to be responsible, how to manage my time
I want to thank everyone, teachers, friends, and classmates, big time
They helped me develop myself into the person I am today
They helped me flourish and thrive in every single way
Thank you school, you taught me my skills and my tools
And now, after an amazing journey, I'm off to high school

Emotions
by Keana Roberts

It causes all the commotion,
They can make us broken,
Or make us golden,
What puts everything in motion,
It makes us who we are,
Some might say we're bizarre,
But I think we are like stars,
And like scars,
Emotions last forever.

Cat Teachers
by Luke Ashman

What if my teachers were cats?
Maybe I could get them little hats
But I might not learn much trigonometry
But I could learn how to be lazy
Would it be good if my teachers were cats?
If they were, it'll be as useless as a television class
I think it would be better if they were human
Maybe I could learn about the Constitution
Cats are no good teachers
Just like many creatures
Teachers are one of a kind
It's the only way we can coincide

Time
by Joel Stankiewicz

The world has attempted to measure time
It measures time using days, months, and years
By a calendar
It measures time using seconds, minutes, and hours
By a clock
But it truly cannot be measured
Time is a river
It never stands still
Time flies like a bird
And travels slowly like a snail
Time is without beginning
And without end
My time is measured by God
Time is infinite

High Tide, Low Tide
by Fox Caminiti

flourishing tides
i reside.
with water, so controlled, so plentiful
i take my time.
sunrise anew
i ensue.
school starts
i'm full.
school ends
i'm fine.
but homework ...
i'm empty and dry.
bottomless crater
i plea to leave.
with water, long since evaporated
i rush and plead.
sunrise anew
i refuse.

The Path
by Joseph Laudo

And so the winding path has come to an end
But where one journey ends, another begins
Looking back it's all been a blur
The 9 years I spent here have flashed by
Looking forward, I see another adventure in the distance
My trail continues on.
I know not what the future holds.
It may be dark, it may be bright,
But my journey continues on.
Soon everyone will go their separate ways and some I may never see again
Some continue with me on this path, some don't
But I won't forget them, not one bit.
I grew up with these kids, watched them grow and change.
These three classes of kids have been my world.
They won't slip from my memory anytime soon.
And so the journey ends, the grand journey from kindergarten to eighth.
So much has changed and things will keep changing.
Time marches onward and so do I, on this path of life.

Depression
by Rachel Stewart

I'm depressed not obsessed
I feel oppressed, I want to cry in distress,
I may be blessed but I am just a mess
I guess it's just an endless madness
as I'm filled with sadness, not happiness.
I'm helpless, my eyes filled with dullness.
The evilness is not harmless
it makes me feel loveless and nameless and hopeless,
I might reply in rudeness but that's to replace the sadness.
I may look scarless and be wordless
but that's to hide the ugliness and my weakness.
I am not angerless, I may be brainless
but I have countless nights
as I stay awake with nothing but quietness and darkness
as I lie on my bed, sleepless.
I am consumed in the sinfulness

She Knocks
by Nathan Yowell

The knocking, oh how it plagues my sleep,
Nothing makes me slumber, not even counting sheep
Oh her knocking, she is like all the rest,
She will never be quiet, she is my constant pest
Every step I've taken, she will not be here long,
Silence is coming soon, soon she'll cease her song
But tonight I wish it'd stop, she really is quite loud,
No matter what I do, it's just the constant sound
I yell for her to quiet, her scream is full of fright,
There's a smile on my face, my lone source of delight
She instantly resumes, I spring out of my bed,
Out to the mausoleum, past the long-since dead
I fling the door wide open, she shields her eyes from light.
"You will join your brother, and it will be tonight"
The bag is on her head, I didn't know what I'd done,
I threw her in the grave, now it's time for fun
I start to pile dirt, she makes a muffled scream,
Nothing will stop me now, only the sunlight beam
Now that she is buried, I am full of only scorn,
But families come in daily, and more girls that come to mourn

What If
by Mashonica Evans

What if I had sent that text
And what if he had called
What if I knew what came next
And what if I had stalled
What if people noticed me
But what if people stared
What if I could pay no fee
To have someone I knew cared
What if I could just go back
Be born a different me
What if all the traits I lack
I had for all to see
Would I then be good enough
Would I start to matter
Would I start what-iffing stuff
Return to being shattered
What if I just live for now
And what I can control
Let anxiety take a bow
What ifs be off patrol

I Am
by Kathryn Webb

I am athletic and devoted
I wonder what the crowd is thinking
I hear our fans going wild
I see an upcoming defender
I want to take home the victory
I am athletic and devoted
I pretend to be invisible
I feel like everyone depends on me
I touch the ball with my feet
I worry that I might lose it
I cry at the last whistle
I am athletic and devoted
I understand that both teams can't win
I say "You've got it" over and over again
I dream of the world cup trophy
I try to send the assisting pass
I hope we get the shiny gold trophy
I am athletic and devoted

Change
by Anna Taylor

Why do I put up with the ones who hurt me the most
The ones I call my friends
The ones who act like I'm a ghost
The ones who scream at me to shut up
The ones who might have believed in me once
I trudge through each day like salmon in the current
Trying to keep a smile through my fears
Every day I cry out for help
The only one to answer is my tears
I hide everything from everyone
Becoming more confused than a midnight sun
For what else can you do when no one's willing to listen
When the apocalypse is already in ignition
Filled with people trapped in a popularity prison
Filled with times when kindness is a rarity
Filled with people who donate to their own fake charities
Filled with people who don't even know they're being torn apart
There is no way out of the deep hole in my heart
I just hope that I don't cave in
I guess all I can do is count on time and wait for my coffin

My Journey Through 8th Grade
by Holland G.W. Quinn

Here at St. Theresa has been a nine year roller coaster;
a time full of ups and downs.
When you are scared and are folded in like a flower bud,
It tells you to open yourself up to the world.
When your new and old friends talk to you, the school does too.
It tells you not to give up and stand for yourself.
When it seems like life has smacked you in the face,
It tells you that you can always turn back to your friends here.
When you feel like screaming at nothing and everything,
It holds you and tells you that it's going to be okay, even if it isn't.
When you are looking for some silly times where you can just laugh,
It tells you to join in the fun.
When you finally say goodbye to the place you practically grew up,
It gives you a cheerful wave and tells you to keep growing strong.
When you turn your back with all your friends
on the place where you grew up together,
It turns and welcomes another generation of friends.

Colors of Life
by Amelia Schmidt

red, green, yellow, blue
colors of life, which one to choose, so many to do
but how I can't see
there's too many colors that remind me of me
I look and I look and all that I see are the colors of life I try not to be
I'm angry, I'm sick, I'm sad, like the colors of life I try not to be
like the colors of life I try not to be
red, green, yellow, blue

No Perfect Me
by Makayla Parkin

When will you see, there's no such thing as a perfect me.
There's no such thing as normal, only unique,
and there's no such thing as perfect, just simply beautiful.
We are all changing, morphing into what we call normal.
A new "more improved" version of ourselves.
More like a copy of what we say is perfection.
I hope you know that an original is better than a copy.
You are you, and you are me? Whoever that may be.
There is nothing more that I want to be than me.
NOT PERFECT,
NOT NORMAL,
NOT A COPY,
Me.

One Step At a Time
by Brianna Manni

one step at a time,
don't go too fast,
always trying to beat everyone else,
jumping to conclusions,
no one has ever made it far,
taking one step,
you have to take more than one step,
in order to get to the top,
sometimes slow is enough,
savor the good times like it's your favorite food,
take your time,
enjoy it with the people you love,
don't take them for granted,
you never really appreciate them until they are gone.

Hope
by Cristina Vasquez

Hope is the candle which will never burn out
Hope is the little girl who helps you get back up when you fall
Hope is the bird that keeps flying high through all its hardships
Hope is the star that shines at night
Hope is just your simple friend who won't let you down
Hope is the rose you see in the garden you walk by
Hope is the puppy who brings you joy
Hope is the butterfly that flies around all the flowers
Hope is the waterfall that travels a long way and remains beautiful
Hope is the light that shines bright
Hope will bring change in the world and your life,
never give up hope even in the hardest of times

Time
by Brendan Baron

Time
It ticks away nonstop
Never slowing down, never speeding up
The clock moves his hand slower than a snail,
Yet everyone's days of youth slowly melt away like a snowflake
Whenever you look back, everything seems like it just happened yesterday
And centuries ago at the same time
Time flies by like a commuter late to work
Before we know it, we're as old as the stars
If only we had more time
Then we could do more things and go more places
If only we had more time

Apiology: a Study of Honey Bees
by Carly Yates

Mean girls swarm like angry bees.
A cranky queen makes for a hostile hive.
It's hard to resist their honey,
But their stingers come with barbs and hooks,
They don't crawl away to die after.
Watching from a distance, I hear their infernal chatter.
Beating wings, discontent and disillusioned
I offer nothing sweet for them to feed on.
Astonished looks, entranced by their golden nectar.
Mindlessly adding to their colony that slowly collapses.
I long to set them free from their little wooden box
So small, yet all consuming.

Football
by Julian Powell

The sport of football
Always make the tackle
The love for the game

Military Brat
by JaKayla James

The three years are gone
Time to go
My life's no happy song
Away we go to the next town we know
I might even go overseas
It's too bad no one will know me
I start over every year
None of my friends ever stay near
To left and right, new faces around
From everyone I get a frown
Three years are gone
It's time to go
It was nice knowing everyone
It was fun
But now I'm done
Hopefully, I'll meet someone

What If
by Erin Cain

What if I went to a different school
And didn't believe in God.
What if I had a different teacher
Like Mrs. Krumel, Mrs. Settar or Mrs. McDonald.
What if on the first day,
I decided to talk to someone else.
Would I have the same friends I have now?
What if my friends today were my enemies.
What if I had chosen to love as Jesus loved me.
Maybe I should have become friends with the kid who sat alone at lunch.
What if I had actually read the textbook pages for homework
Or studied a little harder for that math quiz.
What if I never agreed to go to this school.
Would I be prepared to go live my life?
Life is a roller coaster, without school would I know how it works?
I am not proud of all the choices I have made, but I am glad I made them.

Sunflowers
by Heather Pearson

Nothing is so beautiful and fun,
As a sunflower looking to the sun.
They face that way only to survive,
But it still surprises people as they watch them thrive.
It is even better if you can see them bloom,
From the window in your own bedroom.
Sunflowers are often called rings of fire,
And are magnificent plants many people desire.

In-Between Thoughts
by Stella Kluth

He's here now I notice, the guest of the hour,
The man who will steal my dreams.
Yet while stealing my dreams he shall save me from nightmares,
a good man at heart it seems.
Slowly I remember of times, feelings of joy, memories of love,
a lifetime of family and friends.
Slowly I remember of times, feelings of fear, memories of sadness,
a lifetime of misery and regret.
As I lie here in this bed I go back to the time it happened.
The night with a devil's sound, a flash of light,
My scream cutting through darkness as the car goes by.
He's here now I think, smiling my cheeks go rosy pink,
my enemy, my friend, my hero.
He's here now I feel relieved, the man who will take me away
my past, my future, my end.
I'm here now, he speaks, you can call me Death.

Lazy Angels
by Atilia Thomas

We're the lazy ones, the ones that simply watch, never protect.
We watch from above the rooftops and the clouds,
all having our own child to watch.
Watch as they grow into teens, they start to dream about
the latest Gucci handbags and their crushes at school.
We watch as they do drugs and get into fights.
We warn them to watch and be careful, but it is them who choose to listen.
We simply watch, never protect.
We watch as they grow into adults.
Watch as they make the wrong decision after decision after decision.
We warn them, we warn them, we warn them.
But they never listen 'til it's over.

Mother Nature's Deadly Trio
by Ty Earley

Fast spiraling wind
Everything in sight destroyed
Evacuate now
Comes with no warning
Throws houses around like toys
Better take cover
Mountain with fire
Throwing up like a dragon
Making hell on Earth

Knocking
by Aidan J. Hamilton

There is knocking.
Feeling and sounding urgent, the shocking overwhelming knocking.
It is rhythmatic, as if a heartbeat, beating fast... jolting, duh duh... duh duh.
It comes from one point, one space, one influencer.
Although, I feel it compacting me from all sides.
I am scared, so I start pondering the choice of locking the door
to block the shocking knocking from occurring anymore.
Although, I know who is there at the door.
It has popped up much in my life before.
And it has knocked so many more times than a mortal could harbor.
And every appearance of it I have ignored.
And to consider the possible positive position I could be in today,
could have rocked me like ships sailing over ocean waves
whooshing wildly, to not ignore it.
I feel an overpowering form of remorse I know I am responsible for considering it
was constructed from my home-grown loads of gloomy conclusion possibilities.
But now my remorse retaliates and starts to slowly, steadily, painstakingly, shove me
towards the now new pounding sound from the door.
I fight the pushing, a civil war erupts in my head, with two sides brawling the bold
battle whether to stay or go; remorse or myself.
I then discern my dull reflection reflecting
from the shiny, spotless remorse ridden door.
And I am surprised to see a sea of fallen fulfillment spread over my face
like a white blanket covering a dead body with no success.
That view touched me inside, I was always scared of the shocking knocking, its
urgency and unpredictability, where it could lead.
But now, I come to the realization I can climb out of a hole I have fallen into and
grow stronger from the unpredictable, unthinkable chances
I could score if I just... opened the door.
I opened the door, a beautiful, bountiful beam of hope hit my icy face
I had never felt before.
"Hello Opportunity," I said.

Next Best Thing
by Emma Berry

My mind, it tells me
They cannot love me for long
They grow tired, dancing slows
I am no more than a passing song
Played on the radio for a while
Mediocre at best, they all say
It falls fast out of style,
As if it ever was in style at all
My heart, it tells me
Something inside is broken
Scratched record, stuck in a loop
Everything goes up in flames, smoking
Ratings drop before the mic hits the ground
World is silent, the beat is gone
There never was anything to like about the sound
Everything stops as they forget,
And move on to the next best thing.

Wildflower
by Makayla Kennedy

In the beginning, a seed.
Flying through the air, in a place where no one dared to go.
It planted itself into the ground, sure of what it could be.
Then, a sprout.
Despite the dry, brittle dirt, it grew and flourished.
Rain came through from time to time,
helping the sprout grow and petals thrive.
But then, a storm.
The worst in 20 years.
Wind, rain, hail ... destruction.
The flower, not surrounded by any others, was destroyed.
From the destruction, a new seed.
Not one, not two, but five.
No more severe storms hit.
Light rain and warm conditions ensued.
It gave way to life, and flowers bloomed.
Years later you will be able to go to a place, a wonderful place!
One where life is thriving,
And has a huge field of wildflowers.

Thin Line Between Love and Hate
by Alexa Lopez

Love
Joyful, Beautiful
Satisfying, Fulfilling, Amazing
Heart, Kisses, Punches, Wounds
Fighting, Arguing, Injuring
Harmful, Angry
Hate

Angel of Nature
by Erica Aaron

Nature is a magnificent sight
A newborn is unveiled to this world
To them nature is a new life
For as the newborn the world is evolving
The newborn may have ups and downs
As the newborn is becoming a child
It still thinks of this world as a sanctuary
Only as it is still learning to love and care
When the child sees a butterfly,
The child thinks the butterfly is tranquil
But yet there is always someone there,
In the child's life to lift the child up on
The child's feet and watch him develop,
Into a young man to an adult

Best of Me
by Kelsey Brewer

I saw you on the first of June.
When it had struck the time of noon.
And with a smile and big blue eyes.
It had reminded me of the big blue sky.
With the cool breeze through your hair.
I thought to myself that life was fair.
You came over to me at the seaside
While I felt so much pride.
You asked me if I wanted to go for a walk.
And as we had come across the dock.
You had looked back.
And as you looked back you had seen the tracks.
That we had left.
When you said something that made us laugh.
That was the time you could see.
The best of me.

Family
by Sage Thompson

Family is like a puzzle
A family has all kinds of pieces
Everybody has a part when it comes to family
If everybody stays together, and sticks like glue,
it won't come apart, and that's family.

Life
by Kailee DiRienzo

I am light, and I am dark,
I am the thing that can tear you apart,
I am fragile, but I am strong,
I am the Thing That Rules All,
I am breathing, and I am living,
I am seeing, and I am sensing,
I am small, but I am large,
So what, pray tell, am I?
For I am Life!

True Side
by Hays Turner

I never planned who I was going to be.
Most people only know 1 side of me. Only a few know my true side.
Everyone has 2 sides.
Only giving a key to special people in life to unlock your true side.
My other side is a mask to cover my true side.
The side that is not athletic, but tries,
a good student, but also likes archery and target shooting.
Driving down dirt roads in my dad's jeep
that is raised & loud so you can hear it miles away
While singing Copperhead Road, Take Me Home Country Roads,
and Amazing Grace.
I am a tomboy one day and then the next a girly girl.
I act like I know today's hits, but I am stuck in the 80s like quicksand
and I can't get out.
Breathing old time rock & roll. Living in Broadway musicals.
I know the word to every play old and new.
Growing up singing Greased Lightning every night before bed
and dancing with Danny Zuko. Seeing Grease at the age of 4.
This is my true side not my fake.
The fake side acting like everyone else just to fit in and look normal.
No one is normal or perfect.
Watch out, I am taking off my mask.

Big Brother
by Jessica Wold

Thinking about you kills me.
Thinking about all the memories kills me.
Thinking that I now have to face this alone kills me.
It feels like you're a million oceans away and I'm just barely floating.

Broken Soul
by Olivia Malone

You sit and wonder
Suddenly, flashes and thoughts
They come and haunt you
Leaving you to be afraid
A broken soul is all that's left
Left with bad memories
There is light and all you have to do
Is take your mind there
Leave the thoughts, the flashes
and the haunting, the fears
Leave the broken soul and come to the light
Your soul will bring you back to the dark
Scaring you
But leave it, leave the broken soul
And go
Go to the light

Her
by Natalie Mahler

Her family celebrated my birthday.
Her mother bought me a cake.
Her sisters sang to me.
It's 2 AM and I can't sleep because I've been shouting poetry at her
in a way to express my feelings towards her.
There are words that I want to scream from a mountaintop
in hopes that she'll care after she's heard them.
There are words I want her to soak in, like paint on a brush.
But then I remember. That this is reality; a place where I cannot just say
a few simple words and everyone treats it like an everyday thing.
Tonight she was upset.
About life.
About people.
About things that I could do nothing about
so instead I screamed lyrics at her, hoping they would reach her
across this big blue ocean we call life.

Determination
by Brooke Lampton

It's the beginning of SUCCESS
Not a PROCESS
It's something that you have
Not something that is GIVEN
It's got the power to PULL you FORWARD

Friend
by Amaya Bennett

You make me happy
You make me cry
With tears of joy
Our love will never die
You're my life
You're my heart
We will always be together
We will never part
I am proud to call you my friend
Because you are always there
Even when I need advice
Or don't know what to wear
Sad to say
Our lives may end
It was great to know
I had a friend

The Ocean
by Carlos Vazquez

From the surface near the land
To the deep blue with the sand
Exploring nature's caverns in the dark
And shipwrecks and mines in a spark
Schools of fish living in coral reefs
Plants of all kinds lacking structural leafs
Sea stars, sea urchins, and sand dollars all alike
Sharks, dolphins, and whales so lifelike
Discovering new species from deep within
Including where others may have been
Afraid that your oxygen may run out
Even if you don't have a single doubt
The ocean is such a wondrous place
So unique and similar to space
That is why we must protect it
And if we do we can all benefit

Shaking the Moon
by Eva Hays

"Careful, you're shaking the moon," she whispered
as the darkness swept me off my feet
Lost me in its gaping depths, pinpricks of light blinding each one
Making shapes, corners, and crevices
and I squint despite the clarity
because it is hard to grasp the gravity of it all
Pinning me, spinning, my head is spinning
I feel smaller than the stars
Maybe someday I will shake the moon

The Telltale Heart
by Maggie Beach

Nothing ever happens in this old town
Until the man's vulture eye made me frown.
I will destroy that eye, I swear
He is completely unaware.
For seven nights at the opposite of noon
I stealthily creeped into the man's dark room.
But then on the eighth night
The old man shrieked in fright.
I saw the vulture's eye
Then felt he had to die.
The police came over and I took a seat,
Soon beginning to hear the old man's heartbeat.
- Inspired by "The Tell-Tale Heart" by Edgar Allan Poe

Living the Dream
by Amelia Gunnufson

My dream is basketball,
you have to be strong
in the head and the heart.
My dream,
I count dunks instead of sheep.
When I step on the court,
I get butterflies swirling around in my stomach.
Living the dream,
my sister, my friends, and my parents
got me hooked on this sport.
Living the dream,
waking up knowing
my basketball dream has come to life,
knowing my family and friends are here
to help me get better

Smokescreen
by MacKenzie Kerr

Black virus encrusted society
Produced by man,
Shifty figurehead, sightless mankind
To be bought by man,
Labeled multitudes, open forgery
Then molded and broken by man,
Decomposing culture, dead camaraderie
Forming you into a single piece of waste
To be thrown out
Smokescreen to your social order

Everything's Fine
by Rylee Smith

My eyes start to blur,
My words start to slur,
I can't breathe, yet you're fine,
You're saying there is always time.
You're always on my brain,
And yet, you're so tame.
So many days have gone by,
And I still can't stop asking why.
The flames have now died,
And since then my spirits have arisen.
Everything is fine.
There will always be time.

The Past
by Kathleen Steward

I hate saying goodbye. This simple word stabs your heart like a dagger.
This word bends your world like a hammer to a nail.
This word burns deep in your everything as a fire burns paper.
This word makes you cry like you have never cried before.
This word tears you up like a torn letter.
But then there are the other meanings of goodbye.
Goodbye can mean it's time to start over.
Goodbye can mean it's time to move on.
Goodbye can mean let's put the past behind us.
We try to move on and it's hard for awhile.
But your heart will heal with time.
Your world will be bent back into place. The fire will be put out.
Your tears will dry. You will be ok again.
I hate saying goodbye but I know I need to in order to move on.

Depression
by Kelly Blancett

Sadness is seen as an evil thing
With claws and jaws that snap the mind.
But sadness is not some great beast
Waiting for any weakness it can find.
It is merely a companion to comfort us
In our times of hardship and need.
It lets out our side that doesn't agree
With the veil of our shell of society.
Sadness is seen as an evil thing
With a twisted sense of self.
But sadness is not something to fear
Not when it brings such calming wealth.
It breaks our chains of ill-gotten gains
And helps our hearts to mend.
The mind is not so easy to break
When we know sadness as a friend.

Reincarnation
by Shailee Sran

what if when they said energy cannot be created or destroyed,
it meant something more
if the universe is a circle, self-contained in every aspect,
and not an atom goes to waste, then:
how many of our souls are recycled?
imagine a god that it is not a god of life or death;
a being that reshapes lives, is all
this creature must smear a thousand unspoken words
across their skin
and a death (a life) becomes a cupped blue egg in their hands.
their skin is water and mother's milk (the sea)
and their blood is starlight. see,
what if we are immortal - what if years and years ago,
when the stars formed our bodies, they gifted us with the ability
to die like stars die. to recollect our beings in something different.
star to galaxy to planet.
then: there was never a period at the end of our sentence,
never a question with poetry
and the essence of humanity curled into the punctuation.
what if we are a circle that gains nothing and loses nothing?
(how tired this creature must be.)

My Name
by Amina Hashi

Awesome.
Marvelous.
Incredible.
kNows a lot of things.
Appreciable.

The Big White House
by Sophia Rossen

Whoever lives in the big white house
Seems to control the brain of every innocent mouse
Feeding them fake milk and cheese
Why do they always have to tease?
Other mice want a chance to be free
The cat in the house closes them off with big ol' trees
Different mice try to talk
The cat in the house only mocks
The mice walk to defeat
The cat laughs and stands to his feet
No one knows when it will end
For now the mice will just have to take a stance

Time Unravels
by Cooper Reed

Time unravels before my own eyes,
it leaves in its wake so much surprise.
A mischievous little monster unwilling to compromise,
joining you without warning hoping you will mess up and capsize.
You may try to stop him if you are wise,
though if you fail he'll claim you as a prize.
Time is the ultimate ending for everything in the world,
if you think about it it's as if we are in a dream world.
The one with all the strings, the almighty one,
a man with a bullet, you cannot outrun.
A thief with your wallet of precious memories,
of times not forgotten, but lost in the strong breeze.
I as a human, rebel against its will,
though to Time I'm nothing, but a tiny meek krill.
I can't control Time as it unravels before my eyes,
So I guess I just have to live as Time's little meek prize.

Just a Dream?
by Coral Standke

I felt the green grass sliding through my toes like wet sand.
I could hear the mockingbird singing its sweet songs like slow jazz music.
I tasted the blue air that drenched me like pouring rain.
I saw nothing; pitch black.
I reached out, but you weren't there.
My legs went numb and my eyes melted.
I turned around and there you were.
Smiling with your precious blue eyes.
Blood was running down your cheek.
I woke up looking at a girl in a hospital bed.
A boy with blue eyes yelled, "Wake up, Eleanor."
The machine was buzzing like bees.
The blue-eyed boy ran out of the room.
I walked up to the girl and touched her red hair.
I woke up lying in a hospital bed.
A boy with blue eyes was crying and holding my hand.
He whispered, "Eleanor, I love you."
I whispered back, "I love you more."

My Love
by Mallory Hass

As blades cut through my fingertips
The adrenalin flies
As the crowd screamed
All I could think of was him
The crowd sang along to words they don't understand
My Love, my only Love, at home
Smiles, oh smiles erupt as he shows his face
Making my day shine brighter than the sun
My Love, my only Love, with me
But our smiles didn't last long
As rain washed away the dust
As clouds covered the sky
The adrenaline still flew, and my fingers bled
The devil had taken control to steal our souls
Oh the lives he will ruin by stealing my Love, oh my soul
The crowd sang along unfazed as I watched the lights in his eyes
My Love wanting more but couldn't receive
A hero shall rise, before we die, to save us again
My Love, my only Love, will be with me again

Piano
by Greta Pfeifer

Life is like a piano.
That's what people tell me.
You should be happy, you play such a beautiful instrument.
You can play anything you want, this is a skill you can use your whole life.
It will help you get into college, get a job, this is great.
They always tell me I play so well.
You have the skill you just don't have the passion.
Someday you will love it if you just stick with it.
Maybe someday I will love it,
Life is like a piano.

The You In Me
by Lydia Gillis

As they all depart and go their ways, I'm going to sit here and look at you
I wish I could hold your hand and stay and say what I want to say and do
You inspired me to dance and sing, you told me your tales of the war
You told me about everything, I should have asked you more
As everyone cries and walks away, I'll stay with you till the end
I recall those after-school days when I climbed in every tree's bend
And you called to say it was supper time,
I couldn't wait to warm by fireside
We'd watch Disney films, past bedtime,
we'd both cry so hard when Bambi's mother died
Oh, how you complained about those trees,
how they needed to go, they made you frown
Now I stand there, see them swaying in the breeze,
I just can't bring myself to cut them down
I can still see you standing in the window,
waving goodbye as we pull out of the drive
When I was young and just a little fellow,
I never thought there'd ever be a last time
That's why I'm crying now, thinking of everything I took for granted
The look in your eyes the last time I saw you,
your hands held mine, your fingers so slanted
So I'm going to sit here and look at you, for this is the last moment I have
I'm going to say what I want to say and do,
for one last time, I wish I could hold your hand
Everyone has said goodbye so I guess it's now my turn
I'm not going to leave and cry, no, I want to give you what I learned
I learned to dance, sing and more,
to keep my head held high, even if tears fall to the floor
Because I now know what I'm going to do ...
Grandma, I'm going to be like you

A Lifestyle Less Chosen
by Hannah Shupe

Music, what do you think?
Melanie Martinez, Twenty One Pilots, Drake, something along those lines
What do I think? What do you think I think?
You see, I don't think what you think I think
Heavy metal, death, those are the words you expect me to spill from my lips
When you ask me music
But what if I told you I was a little more open-minded than that?
And hopefully you'll be too, when I hear someone say music
Death metal, alternative metal, heavy metal, thrash metal, black metal, rock
Of course, that's what you expect, but today, I think not
Today, I think lifestyles, for music is not just song and sound
Music is not just a finger tap
Music is not just a so-called "artist" wearing a so-called "style" on TV
Music, music is a lifestyle, it's who you are
Country, well-made cowboy hats and cowboy boots and real leather
My dad likes country music, you know
My brother and I got him a cowboy hat a few years back
He still wears it every once in a while
Metal, I know what you think that is
Gargling lyrics that you can't understand, screeching guitars with no rhythm
It's all trash ... to you, I know what you think we are
Black, ugly attire, watching you in despise, death on our minds, violence
Pentagrams everywhere for us to worship the unholy one down below
Hating in silence, we're all trash ... to you
I'm here to tell you otherwise, I'm here to tell you the truth
I can only hope that you listen, all that I ask is that you listen
And hope what I'm saying can get through to you
What if I told you that hidden in those ferocious words, those growling lyrics
Was a meaning, an important one
That if you really listen, you can hear them speak, understand the words
And find that the person behind those deep tones is trying to make a statement
Is trying to have a voice. No talent, you say? Well what if I told you that
A man once could not speak until he was onstage because if he did,
he might lose his voice, because the vocals put such a strain on his voice
What if I told you that some of those wild guitar notes are so complicated
and quick and strong that those who achieve mastering it are dubbed legends
That these songs, voices, notes can take years to master
And that some can't even do it at all
What do you want me to say? "Yes, I worship Satan"
Probably what you were expecting, no
What if I told you that Christian metal is a well-liked metal subgenre
That I go to church every other Sunday with my grandma
And what if I told you that fighting is always my last resort
That I love my family and friends just as much as you do
That I won't hate you, I won't hurt you
So I don't understand why you treat us this way
Why you deny us, ignore us, treat us this way, we're not different, we're human
We don't judge you by what you wear and what you listen to
So why do you judge us?
We may look and sound intimidating, but if you really get to know us,
If you open your mind and try, then so will we, because of this we are loyal and true
Because we know the value of having someone to love and that loves you
And what if I told you that I have a Johnny Cash t-shirt at home in my drawer
And I am proud to say, that I chose a lifestyle less chosen

The Time Ticking Alpines
by Anna McCabe

The mountainous breeze bites at my frosted face,
Snow drifts by, blinding my vision.
My dad glances to his wrinkled wrist,
Informing us, we've been wandering the desolate alpines for nearly three hours.
Crystalline snowflakes dance together, piling up along the abundant tree branches.
My mom starts to topple, frightening the forested land.
My skin is raw to the bone,
The aroma of pine trees enlighten my nose.
We desperately cry for help, but all I hear is the whistling wind.
Solutions slowly go through my clouded mind.
A ruby red sled appears next to me, as if it was there all along.
I struggle to turn my head to my unconscious family.
My breath echoes in my head.
Energy sinks through me climbing on the glistening sled,
Riding my way to freedom.

Characteristics of Autumn
by Naomi Gertz

Leaves are turning, brilliant, bright
Elegant unto my sight
Anchored strong onto a tree
Falling, swirling, then on me
Wind comes blowing from the west
Irritating me at rest
Nodding branches bow to him
Dancing, bending, leaf and limb
Mugs of cider, cocoa, chai
Useful with a slice of pie
Great for freezing autumn nights
Saving me from cold that bites
Fire leaps within its crate
Inching over wooden freight
Reaching up to warm my face
Etching "home" into this place
Fall is knocking at my door
Asking me for room to soar
Letting go to summer's grip
Leaving me to run and skip

3rd Place

Erin Chalk

Floraison
by Erin Chalk

A blank page stares at me,
Waiting. Watching.
I stare back.
A horizon line splits the page,
Earth and sky.
Mountains reach for the heavens,
Always falling short.
Rivers snake across the ground,
Being devoured by the ocean.
A sapling is planted,
Cradled by the earth,
Nurtured by the light.
The sky clears, and the sun brushes the
Ground, coaxing.
And the sapling
Blooms.
A full page smiles at me,
Sleepy and content.
I smile back.
Satisfaction.

2nd Place

Katherine Milner

The Break of Winter
by Katherine Milner

An icy breath upon winter's crest;
The frosty wind, slicing through the air,
The taste of revenge and fury
Protruding from its gelid lips.
Like a frozen dagger, an icicle
Hangs above my head.
Warning me to step away
Else I feel its frigid wrath.
And watch it take its journey,
Down towards the final shattering
That I seem to hear ringing
In my ears this very moment.
Cold as a shiver down a petrified spine
The flakes of ice and snow crystallize.
Descending from the clouds, these arctic ornaments
Put many into its trance of everlasting fascination.
Out of the wintry woods stroll frost-coated deer,
The chilling glacial winds nipping sharply at their heels.
The trees, lightly dusted with snow,
Signify that winter has begun.

1st Place

Molly House

Molly was a ninth grade student
when she entered her poem,
"American Pie" in our national contest.
Her love for reading seems to be surpassed
only by her talent for writing.
Excellent work, Molly!

American Pie
by Molly House

Cold hands,
warm heart.
Chunks of fat sitting, ugly,
glutinous in my pretty dough.
The intoxicating aroma of comfort,
of summer evenings,
wafts throughout this privilege.
Layers; flaky and finicky,
I took a step back to achieve these.
I watched and learned and let go
cold hands,
as they say.
White pickets and iridescent red apples,
anxious murmurs and flour caked aprons.
Little burns decorating my fingers,
dreams decorating my words,
floating above this house.
Cold hands,
and American pie.

Division IV

Grades 10-12

Trichotillomania
by Kaitlyn Wells

Trichotillomania
Oh how you drive me insania
I plucked and pulled and poked
Now it's nothing but a joke
This is no trick
I do not pick
Trichotillomania
Oh how you drive me insania
You treated me like clay
Never let me play
You took your hold
Never let me loose of the mold
I took a stand for me
A team never were we
Trichotillomania
Oh how you drove me insania

If the Streets Could Talk
by Molly Anderson

If the streets could talk
The whispering would be unbearable
Incoherent mumbling
Would fill the ears of wandering passersby
Making it hard to hear any life nearby
If the streets could talk
No one would walk them
Needless information– clothes, drama, hairstyles
Would spill out of the pavement
And into the hearts of nobody
If the streets could talk
Blood would seep out of the cobblestone
Inconsolable, desperate pleads
Would fog the minds
Of the weary drivers
If the streets could talk
They wouldn't
They'd stay silent
They'd let the people who walk them
Speak for themselves

At a Glimpse
by Brandi Bandel

At a glimpse
I may not look like much.
I can be small or big.
Heights don't faze me
because I fall for miles.
I can be rough or calm,
it depends on the day.
I'm a part of a lot, including you.
I don't need you
but you need me.

Enemy Guns
by Brianna Saylor

Wars should have never been started,
The things soldiers had to endure never leave them lighthearted.
The sadness that sweeps over loved ones
when they find out what happened to their son because of the enemy guns.
The soldiers that risk it all to be brave,
or the ones who cannot handle it anymore and they cave.
These are the reasons why wars shouldn't be started,
because no one can take the consequences wholehearted.

Element
by Elise Clonts

He is made of smoke and ash
But you will never see a cigarette between his fingers
His quiet smiles are full of velvet
But you will find a missing piece of ivory
His eyes are up to the brim with river water
But the moon does not affect their tide
His ebony yarn hair curls at the nape of his neck
But you will find no finer silk in China
His bones are made of steel
But they have been shattered like stained glass
His skin is softer than pebbles
But the clouds are too harsh
His heart is made of beechwood
Salty, weathered and splintered
But someday
A carpenter will walk past
And it will be made more smooth than air

Recall
by Brianna Jenkins

All of the little things floating through time
Stepped over, unnoticed
Until the sponge in my head slurps them up
Packs it away, tucking the numerous keys into its pocket
Whistling while it works, dashing from place to place
Never quite in the right place at the right time
Always scrambling and distressed,
attempting to seal in its grip on the bits and pieces
Before the nature of the beast lets it escape out the other ear
While praying that, when it came to it,
it would remember to let loose the royalty when called
Not that such remembrance matters
It forgot to lock the door

It Was Always Me
by Paryn Masters

Maybe the problem was never they
But rather always me
I seek safety in other spirits
So I can experience release.
I'm just a structure pumping blood
Merely a feeble, detached liar
My small hands clutched at burning hearts
And screamed tirades when I caught fire
My mind, an obfuscated web,
Entangles all those that I need
They vanish in the night sometime,
But I knew someday they'd flee.
I'm a charlatan with my looks
And a siren with my songs
I pray for hearts to take me up
Despite that I'm everlastingly wrong.
I blamed the brave that beheld me
Their earthen eyes growing with fear
For my soul is encased in thorns
Warding off all those who draw near.
I am the utmost forcible
Fragile woman you ever saw
A pair of paradoxes would we make
If one stayed, even through it all.
Maybe someday when I'm older,
And the fog, the blaze, it clears
Will I catch the real culprit
When I gaze into the mirror.

Specter
by Josh Mitrenga

A Specter can't exist without a sight to behold
With the celestial bliss of a dream
the relationship was envisioned
Enveloped in death's stillness
He waited for her
But the news of her passing couldn't be handled
Breathless and cold loneliness crept in
And continued to break his heart with memories of her
Broken by the gap
The Specter reaches in his past for comfort
Without the relief of repetition
A Specter sinks in the ocean
Where love is just ephemeral ecstasy
The place where preconceptions of joy disintegrate and stain his heart
When put under the weight of reality
Waves of heartbreak crash against him
While the compassionate comfort of company ceases to be
So he drifts till the waters take him under
Closing both eyes of the beholder ceases transcendence

Fresh Blues Stuck Together With Duct Tape Under the Coffee Table
by Ariana E. Young

So you read 'em and weep.
Dancin' in the hard plastic seat.
Coffee music, coffee time- blues' not gone- it's here and alive.
You jig and shake,
Not a care in the world when the music gets louder,
Not a feeling in your heart when the groove gets faster.
There's a beat in your heart
And it aches like crazy.
There's tape on your mouth and a Band-Aid on your soul
Boy, it feels good to be far from home.
The mom's crying, the dad's run away.
And it feels like there's nothing telling you to stay;
God, it feels good to be full of blues.
Shake to the music, a fresh heartbeat that's erratic in speed
No coffee in the world could help this beat bang harder.
A snap of your fingers- or was it your heart?
Who cares, man- party's already started,
And you're not the only one leaving here brokenhearted.
So think about- about the dirty deeds being done dirt cheap.
As caffeine soda-pop tears spill from your eyes and into your cup

My Wonderland
by Erika Jutton

There was a time when I lived in a Wonderland
Running with Alice and the Cat
My life was grand; I had no plans
Then one day you came
You were worse than the Queen of Hearts
I fell in something that I knew wasn't love
I lost my head
I pitied you so I stayed
And in return you broke me down
I was too naïve to leave
You were wrong to treat me that way
Now I keep going, I'm getting stronger every day
I can live without you, that's what I keep showing
I'll return to my Wonderland with the Rabbit and the Cat
I've found my own heart
I've got all the time in Wonderland
I'm growing up, I'm getting stronger
I'll never shrink again
Overcoming everything
Living in my Wonderland

The Ship
by Madeline Skrukrud

The ship's sail billowed in the soft winds.
Waves lapping against the hull of the sailboat.
Laughter comes from the people on the shore
watching the sailboat peacefully go by.
The laughter slowly fades as the sailboat drifts farther out to sea.
Slowly the bright cloudless sky gains clouds and the clouds turn darker.
At the same time the sun starts to fade, leaving its last kisses behind.
Winds harden, the sail flails.
With the winds come rougher waves hitting against the hull.
Each raindrop like a punch to the sail and deck.
Water splashes onto the deck. Filling it slowly.
In the distance rocks start to form and take shape
into jagged peaks along the horizon.
The storm laughs a thunderous laugh at the boat's impending doom.
As the rocks get closer the storm gets quieter.
The sailboat goes back to its peaceful state.
The winds change and slowly it returns back to where it started.
Little Johnny picks up his toy boat from the bath
and returns it to the shelf where its next adventure is waiting.

I Can't
by Iyanna Tucker

Feeling my lungs cave in, trying to catch my breath
Lights flashing towards my face,
looking for the words to come out of my mouth
All I could see eyes looking before me
As I finally try to speak, fumbling over my words
until I took a deep breath, started again and something started to come out
I was surprised, my eyes started to light up again
There was hope that I could finish
Then I got right down to business
Clapping all over the building
My lungs released, the sweats from my palms stopped
I walked back to my seat
Only realizing that I could achieve with leaving fear behind me
I only had to guide me to find what was inside of me

Peace
by Meredith Farmer

I will close my curtains, I will lock my door.
I will cry and cry until I can no more.
My heart will harden, my feelings will numb,
and somehow I will find peace again.
When I drift into sleep made by pills,
I will realize the rising of the sun kills.
Until then shall I rest, until then shall I rest,
and somehow I will find peace again.
I will open my door and let out a sigh.
I will push forward with my head held high.
"It will be okay," I will say, only a few more hours
and somehow I will find peace again.
As I walk with weight on my shoulder,
not only my heart, but my soul grows colder.
I will keep on walking, I will reach my destination
and somehow I will find peace again.
At last my peace is near, my cheeks now damp with a tear.
I will pick up my pace until I arrive and somehow I will find peace again.
I closed my curtains, I locked my door.
I cried and cried until I could no more.
My heart has hardened, my feelings now numb
and somehow I found peace again.
Peace in shutting my eyes.
Peace in the darkness.
Peace in the absence of mind.

Mirror
by Nina Caldwell

reflection
is the rain
pounding the roof
ruining my brain
running down my face
in the middle
of the drought

Frankenstein's Creature
by Keshaun Wiggins

"Monster, monster," yeah, that's what they call me.
Is it the color of my skin? Is this the reason why I don't fit in?
Or is it the way I walk, maybe the way I talk.
In my heart there is nothing but good, but yet I'm misunderstood.
I sit alone outcast by them all. I just want love but receive none at all.
Verse two is about my pain. A pain caused by society's disdain
which drives me insane. From this insanity grows a huge animosity.
Me versus all. I will be accepted even if I have to kill them all.
If you won't give, then I shall take.
This anger that builds inside is what keeps me awake.
Wait, if I kill them all then who will I date.
I just want love. Love and marriage, it could all be so simple.
But society doesn't accept me like a teenage girl doesn't accept pimples.

Porcelain
by Max McDaniel-Neff

Perfectly pretty, prim and proper
Not a scuff or a mark in sight
Rail-thin legs and big baby eyes
With pretty painted nails and skin of spotless white
Translucent and smooth like porcelain
Perfectly tiny, tiny and perfect,
Are these doll parts crafted with care
For my eyes, and only my eyes
For I am their creator
Full bloated stomach, soggy mush in a gagging mouth
Creating sags and bags and blemishes, get it out, get it out, get it out
I serve my heart on dirty dishes
Perfectly pretty, prim and proper
Not a pocket of fat in sight
Atrophied muscles and dull, dark eyes
With chipped painted nails and skin of dying grey
Fragile and cold like porcelain

No Backup Plan
by Katelyn Stover

No backup plan
No second chance
No bail set to play
In a box in the closet
The names of victims stay
At the tips of my fingers
Their fears never fade
Their cries in the darkness
Amuse me through each pitch
No one can hear me
Sirens pierce my ears
Fear now fills me.

Chocolate-Covered Feet
by Mackenzie Stepp

When I was growing
and, "My, you've grown!"
was nothing,
I ran without a care
and slept with even less;
the people who were evil
with their sharp tongues
who were syrupy sweet
yet smelled like feet
said sharper words,
and the chocolate was good.

I Am No Slave
by Margaret Michel

I work from dusk till dawn.
I work long, very long.
I can't sleep, but I weep.
But I am no slave.
I try and try to run away.
But I can't, so I stay.
I work hard, very hard every day.
But I am no slave.
I cry and I cry.
Hoping someday I'll be free.
Someday I can see the gifts that God has given to me.
I am no slave

In the Embrace of Winter
by Emily Dahlstrom

Found comfort in winter's hold,
Found safety, perched upon my parent's knee.
Found solstice in the days of old.
Found blessed quiet in the cold.
Found sleep, cradled in the crashing sea.
Found comfort in winter's hold.
Found wonder in the shadow's fold,
Found adventure in the winds so free.
Found solstice in the days of old.
Found value in more than gold,
Found friends I trust to be my lee,
Found comfort in winter's hold.
Found faith in stories untold
Found hope in what is yet to be,
Found solstice in the days of old.
Found power in a future, mine to mold.
Found wisdom to cherish every simple glee.
Found comfort in winter's hold,
Found solstice in the days of old.

Where To Go
by Annabelle Foster

Glass in my head scraping the surface
Too many voices having me question if I'm even worth it?
Once a child with a smile
No sense of pain
Nowadays my depression just won't go away
I miss the shine in my eyes
And the way I curled my hair
But I have anxiety-
As if anyone cares
The monster in my closet is still there
But I know what it is now …
My reflection in the mirror
My head is turning
Voice is burning
From swallowing my tears
Silent, but hurting
Once a child with a smile
Now living in fear
Why would you up and leave
When your child is still there

My Experience With Procrastination
by Aidan Eck

It's the reason I fail.
It looms over me like a whale.
It never seems to go away.
It's the reason my mom wants to leave on a sail.
This thing is my temptation.
It is my unhealthy addiction.
I try to stop but I can't.
This thing I speak of is procrastination.
It's just a bad habit,
But I can't seem to nab it.
I have no real reason.
When I finish I think yeah but
Even while sitting in my car,
The journey to the finish is far.
I'm scribbling faster and faster.
It's turning out to be a total disaster.
I'm running out of time.
I've lost the scheme of my rhyme.
Just ten more words left.
Yes! I finally finished it.

The Meaning of Dreaming
by Blaine Olson

What is the meaning of dreaming
Is it just the thoughts in our head
While we sleep in our bed
Or does it have more of a deeper meaning
When we dream of flying oh so high
And seeing all of the shining stars in the sky
We feel as if we could do anything
But in reality we feel
As if we could do nothing
We have forever longed desperately
For that feeling of being free
So in our dreams and in our mind
We all experience something different
Something that is one of a kind
The feeling of being free
Is something different for you and for me
For as long as we are stuck on Earth
Our bodies are trapped on the ground
But when we go to sleep in our bed
We get that feeling of going homebound

The Unknown Lands
by Tiffini Blume

A shadow runs along the ground with wings outstretched
Seconds later colors of red, orange, and yellow flame dance across
Turning bright greens into dark shades of grey and black
The dragon's cry calls out through the air as another spray of fire is spewed
Hooves pound upon the ground with each gracious step
Silvery strands of hair blowing in the wind
Horn sparkling in the light
The unicorn runs in open meadows without a care
Beautiful soft voices sing out
In the mist and perched upon a rock
Vibrant purple and blue scales glitter in the sun
The Sirens are singing their deadly love songs
Once sun goes down and moon rises up
Creatures of day sleep and night creatures wake
Not even in the dark is it truly quiet or still
Howls and barks can be heard
This is a land of mythical, magical, mysterious beings
A land where no human foot could touch
Mystical creatures of all kinds roam
On these lands void of human destruction

Thoughts and Emotions
by Conner Christiansen

Something that you can't explain.
It just sits there up in your brain.
No one will ever understand.
The reason that you stand.
Feeling the weight that isn't there.
People might not even care.
What are you supposed to do.
When there's no one left to turn to.
You try to talk without speaking.
But no one can hear when they're not listening.
You just want to scream.
Because it feels like there's no one on your team.
You try to reason with the darkness inside.
But there is nothing that you haven't tried.
The only one who can hear my silence.
Can only show me guidance.
Who ignited the fire?
Greatness is what I hope to inspire.
If I hope to achieve,
Then I'm going to have to believe.

Rain
by Kayla Brown

The rain fell down from the clouds.
The fluffy, happy clouds.
It fell down onto
the depressed land.
The land deprived of hope,
where dreams are destroyed.
Where no one truly cares.
The rain soaked into the dirt.
Into the lonely dirt
filled with lost dreams
that people gave up.
The rain filled up the holes where the personalities disappeared.
Where the innocence died.
Where joyfulness turned into sadness.
The rain filled the void
Made things better
made things worth it.
The rain gave ideas.
Then all of a sudden
it stopped.

The Meaning of My Katie
by Rhea Schumacher

As I look at my dog so old and gray
She looks as though she cannot play
Her eyes as blue as the great sea
She looks as though she cannot see
Remembering our memories together
You were so miniscule and better
Your fur as black as the night
Your stomach pink and white
Remembering you chasing me
Going on our bike rides so free
Our adventures we had so jointly
As you followed me like a pony
Now you are dreadfully ill
Your back is covered with hills
You walk with great hesitation
Up the steps you proceed with caution
Katie my dog, are you in pain?
You seem as though you are drained
Although you hide it pretty well
I know in my heart you are not well

Meaning of Sports
by Adam Giddings

Sports are cool and fun
There are more than just one
There's soccer, golf, and swimming
Or in baseball with many innings
There is more than just winning.
You may just be in the sport to make friends
Or to spend time till school ends.
But when school ends you can't wait till it starts
Once it starts you don't want it to finish,
If you win you get a beautiful garnish.
You can eat your garnish or wear it well
But don't leave it in the rain or it will swell.
No matter what sport you do
You do it because it matters something to you.
If you end up liking the sport or you are good at it
Try to continue it and not to throw a fit.
You are awesome and the star
Without the factor of how good you are.
If you arrive at practice late
Remember not to absquatulate.

Little Fish
by Moriah Vivone

The saddest thing happened the other day.
My poor fish almost died!
I walked in the kitchen to see the little guy
Only to find he was under the rocks
So I made an attempt to help him out
Trying my hardest to pull him out.
Those rocks had ripped his poor little fin
So now he cannot swim.
A few days have passed and he swims on his side
I'm glad to see he hasn't died.
Every day I give him food
Telling him it will be all good.
This poor little fish I came to love
His black and white colors, those eyes like the skies above
I was washing the dishes with content
I look over and see a little black thing
I walk over to see it was that poor little fish caught in weeds
He could not swim for he had died
The poor little fish that I came to love
Was now in the skies above.

The Child of the Unexpecting Mother
by Maire Dauphine

And so a seed, thus conceived
Be planted in one's heart and veins
For forever this growing feud
shall stay as a part of you
The unexpected
The often relented
As your path is now undetected
And through your thoughts, ye thinks less clearly in demise
Then in a darkened room
More crowded than a rainstorm
With severe pain that ultimately gains
A great achievement is born
It's nurtured by you
It's loved by you
It's cared for endlessly
Then by a single moment ...
all from before becomes a mystery

Aleksandr Solzhenitsyn
by Ryan Grendahl

Born in 1918, into the hands of Lenin's society,
Solzhenitsyn grew up in communism with little piety.
Once accused of criticizing a leader, he spent time in exile,
While in prison, it was books, he would compile.
One of his works, on the use of a Gulag,
The thoughts of prison his mind would jog.
Coming from a home of education and smarts,
Aleksandr would rely on his published arts.
He attended the University of Rostov-na-Donu,
Getting himself in political trouble, he would try not to.
However, he would eventually speak out in Novy Mir, the literary journal,
These works still have their lives, eternal.
Unfortunately, 19 years after the Second World War,
His publishing privileges were shoved in the bottom drawer.
Eventually the KGB would capture his manuscripts,
Thankfully his books would still exist.
In 1970 he was awarded the Nobel Peace Prize,
Due to this, his stardom would only rise.
In 1973, Solzhenitsyn was exiled for the second time,
Even the second time, his reputation was not begrimed.
In 1998, his autobiography was published,
And all five installments would be uplifted.
He would unfortunately perish in 2008,
His greatness nobody can negate.

Jane Austen
by Tiffany Meeks

Her name is Jane Austen.
She wasn't born in Boston.
She was born the 16th of December.
1817 is the year to remember.
For this is the year she passed.
Cassandra was with her till her last.
Cassandra was a true sister.
Harris Wither wanted to be Mr.
She accepted and then declined his proposal.
She threw some of her writings in the trash disposal.
She was as shy as a clam.
Not bold like Uncle Sam.
She wrote and edited six books.
They will have you like hooks.

Love
by Jordan Trombly

Something that cannot be explained.
A feeling only a few people will experience. Overused and imperfect.
Perhaps the only thing science will never discover, for it is too complex.
Hatred and jealousy, so closely related that madness will overtake you.
The rush of seeing them
and the feeling of being so scared to ever lose them.
It will never be explained but that is okay.
Every imperfection and everything that is confusing
is all part of the best feeling one can experience.
For even when it makes us heartbroken, we must never stop searching.
For love, is the best thing we do.

Angel In Disguise
by Cassidy Hansen

She is an angel in disguise– but she doesn't see it with her own eyes
She was sent from Heaven to be on a special mission
It is not always her position– but she doesn't need permission
The Lord above is helping her make the decisions
She prays morning, day, and night
When there is not a soul in sight
She was blessed from a beautiful gift from above
When sharing the word of God– she isn't always preaching
During the late hours of the night– she is reaching–
those that need to be saved
She is an angel in disguise– but she doesn't see it with her own eyes

Nevada the Beautiful
by Rebecca Erkenbrack

See how the Vivid Dancer damselfly goes from flower to flower.
Landing on flowers like sagebrush, a tall beautiful yellow flower.
The mountain bluebird soars overhead, looking down across the ground below.
Where the Lahontan cutthroat trout, swim in the waters of Nevada.
Nevada has Orovada series soil, where flowers and trees grow.
One of the trees is bristlecone pine, a beautiful green pine tree.
The Indian ricegrass grows, in thick green bushes in Nevada.
and the desert bighorn sheep, graze on lush green grass.
These are just a few beautiful things about the Silver and Blue state.
Where their state motto is "All for Our Country," the wonderful Nevada.

The Horns of Sweet Dispatch
by Vincent Wasfaret

The horns of sweet dispatch sound;
No man stands to see the next,
With the tears of despair found,
In the eyes, written in many text;
Of the heart.
From blue to camouflage, smart;
We made a good run,
Now it is time to restart,
From home to the hot dry Arabian sun.
When the bullet riddled, you fell;
forces overtaken,
Terrifying, but all is well,
You have not been forsaken,
Battles lost, but the war is yet justified.

My Escape
by Cammi Cain

This world is becoming horrible
I need to find a way out of this world
I just need to find my escape
I found my escape.
This is my escape, it doesn't have all the bad things
I can finally be myself in this escape that I'm in
This is my escape.
No more wars, and drama.
No more bullies tearing me down, and no more feeling alone in this reality
I found my escape, I'm leaving this reality behind.
This is my escape, it doesn't have all the bad things
I can be myself in this escape I now call home
This is my escape.

Reach
by Ezra Kolle

Reach,
Reach for the ladder.
Reach for the success.
Reach for the cliff edge.
Reach for the safety.
Reach,
With all your might,
With all your fear,
With all your hope,
With all your freedom.
Reach.
The other side is there.
It may be hard,
It may be long,
It may seem impossible.
But the good times are there,
Waiting for you.
Just ...
Reach.

Good News
by Shakara Price

"Slowly, hands shaking with excitement when I open the letter."
It's all about my brother,
He can't cry over milk that spills,
you got to work hard,
until he gets there,
he knows,
he's got to start somewhere,
ever since he hit bottom,
without money,
you can't pay bills,
now he knows the deal,
life isn't easy,
life is so real,
he knows how it feels,
with all his power and will,
he had to work hard,
to get up,
he knew that he was downhill,
he didn't show any tears,
but he was strong!
"Slowly, hands shaking with excitement when I open the letter."

Timothy, the Boy That Cries
by Titus Forseen

Timothy, if I could see you again I would
Timothy, I'm not proud of the life we both have to live
I am just saying I wish you were here
Timothy, I am just saying bye
Timothy, don't cry
Timothy, now you are not alone
Timothy, I just want to say God loves you
Timothy, I cry for you every day
Timothy, don't keep your head down
Timothy, be strong, don't ever give up
Timothy, smile when you are feeling sad

Colored Kids
by Mary Kamara

"Your school called." A girl died. "That's what they said."
I didn't even know her. "Was she sick?" No. It was suicide. "Wow."
I didn't even know her name. "Was she white?"
I walked by her in the hallway.
We worked on the Black History Month display.
She congratulated me on my talent show win.
And I couldn't even bother to learn her name.
"Was she white?" Why do you ask? Why does that matter?
Would that have made a difference? Would it have been easier
to brush it off as something only white people do?
Not the solution for me and you? Is it an easier sentence to swallow
when the crime was committed by the pale and crimson?
Would it be a more comfortable word to digest? Would it have made
your heart any less heavy for the parents whose only child is now gone?
Who will now spend their summers remembering the death of their child,
instead of summering with her in the south of France?
What if she was black? Or Asian? Or Indian? Or Middle Eastern?
What about Mixed? Or Native American?
A seventeen year old girl with a little bit more melanin
hidden underneath her skin? So what if her ancestors owned the slaves?
And so what if they were the slaves? Are these the questions asked?
Are these the answers wanted?
When somebody has chosen to take their own life? What if that was me?
What if the therapy didn't work?
What if the kids were still mean? What if I felt there was nothing else
in the world that could possibly keep me here?
What if somebody asked if I were white?
Would you say yes just so the shame wouldn't cut so deep?
I think to myself, as I quietly respond,
"I don't know, I didn't even know her."

Lovely Words
by Jessica Feick

She is a poem in a world of stories,
Her existence brief but full of meaning.
She lives and breathes complication that piles up
and form her body into taking shape.
She drips love and beauty,
And her eyes that skim her dull, bleak world
are big and full of knowledge and power.
With the flick of a finger,
she flings color onto the gray world that is slowly suffocating her.
She pushes and stretches the tiny box of a world that cannot contain her.

The Perfect Winter Night
by Gabby Ott

The cold, fluffy snowflakes fall around me like feathers,
From a sky as dark as ink, dotted with the falling flakes.
The snowflakes gracefully danced across my skis.
As I nervously stood atop the monstrous hill,
I hear the sounds of skis against the snow,
I see the snowflakes create a crust on the pine trees,
I watch as the new snow covers the old, like sheets on a bed.
The air is filled with snow and I feel the snowflakes landing on my face,
Leaving behind a watery pattern where the snowflakes had melted.
Everything is covered in a calm carpet of pure white.
"Do you want to race me?" my brother asked,
"Of course," I replied, with a smile.

Remember What Is Right
by Dalton Renner

Patriotism is the key,
treat your neighbor as it were you or me.
Never forget who you are,
don't let fame or money shoot you to the stars.
love your family with all you believe,
because this is something to achieve.
pray for the ones from 9/11,
and hope they held onto God and went to Heaven ...
as you do so look to the sky,
in remembrance of the soldiers who have died.
keep a smile on your face,
this is what they would want to embrace.
keep smiling and something great will come,
your war will have already been won.

Death Filled Night
by Jacob Davis

It seems that even sleep has its fees,
As Death's forbidding screams awake me.
Filling me with fears of the past.
His eternal grasp grabs me fast,
Dragging me deep into the darkness so vast.
Which holds no salvation for me,
But eternal peace at long last.
Maybe this is the key,
To me ending the fee,
So Death now guides me.
Don't take Death lightly.

Give Me a Song
by Benjamin Beasley

Give me a taste of a euphoric song,
A presence to save me when all else goes wrong;
A beauty that breaks up the everyday beat,
From the walking and talking--yes, grant me that treat.
Allow me to fly with melodious tunes:
To forests, vast seas, the most distant of moons;
To a babbling brook or the highest of heights,
On the warmest of days or the coldest of nights.
Fill up my heart with the lilt of a voice;
Indulge me with chills that I know aren't my choice.
Leave me in awe with harmonious might;
Then fade away softly--an ending just right.

Untitled
by Savanna Ames

Bright rays of sun God gives to shine on man,
And dulcet fruit for his enjoyment taste,
The meat of trees to harbor and create
And from His breath to write with author's hand.
When Time, that evil foe of all that breathes,
Doth etch the scars of age upon his brow,
And cause to wither every petaled flower
That springs from earth only once more to leave.
What beauty then shall man attempt create
If only to devoured by time be?
Reflections from his glass he cannot keep
Nor from his deathly fate can he escape.
Place not thy hope in things that soon shall fade
But in He outside of time doth stand always.

Will I Ever
by Rachel Barbee

Will my beauty ever mean anything?
Will I ever be enough?
You ignore me like I am insidious
I am a hostage in my own head of black and white images.
Is that all you see of me
You do not see the toxic words you spill
Or my artificial smiles, like I am a doll
Eyes bloodshot red, my soul freshly scraped out, bones, sharp and fragile
My soul scraped sharply, hollower than a rotting tree,
I am covered in bugs, crawling inside of me,
black bugs blindly crawling inside of me.
Falling asleep in the insomnia bed, and eating off the anorexic plate
Your insidious acidic words have made me this way
Alone in a crisp cold room, full of you
losing everyone because they become too oblivious to the pain they create.
To this thing that you call ugly, you will never mean a thing to me again.
Whiter than a piece of copy paper,
with a blade redder than a freshly sliced strawberry.
You have made me this way.
I am a doll with a smile painted on.
Will I ever be enough?

If Only
by Bennett Shane

Here is a glimpse of who I see her to be.
The loyalty, that loyalty was woven of the purest moonbeams,
The very moonbeams that form a soldier's inner seams
And guide him onward in loyalty to his country's dreams.
The trust, earned by those truly deserving,
was crafted from unbreakable stones,
The very stones used by kings to build inspiring monuments and thrones.
The unique intelligence harnessed from the depths of the abyss,
Intelligence leaked down when the greatest fell, the dearly missed.
The wonderful freedom of her spirit expertly siphoned,
siphoned straight from the wind, the wild and free running wind,
Free to go from land to land, bound by none, without end.
The joy, a gift from God's angels bestowed on her.
For only the angels know true joy and when to share.
These individual characteristics have been bound together still,
and held inside by an unrelenting will.
This defining bundle has been tried, tempered, refined, and hardened,
Till it became a thing of gold, stronger than diamonds,
and more beautiful than this world's gentlest sounds.
This extraordinary identity, and her loving features, form her.

Bipolar
by Peter Kistler

Her waves, the Sea believes, are unrefined:
she always must conduct a cleansing tide,
every pull of the sanding surface
roughing clean another harsh imperfection
She always changes her mind, she finds a friendly Child, hello!
Reaching out, his toes touch hers,
and they both run away, chilled. Embarrassed.
She runs back, another extraverted current,
then resigns, embarrassed once more. She does not try again;
she grows ashamed, and sulks away, leaving her tears in the sand.
Her almost Friend picks one out and keeps it safe in his pocket.
At night she comes closer, since Scarers then sleep,
and turns over and over accounts of the day
the most minimal she makes significant,
for she always remembers all of her missteps she records;
not to learn, but to lament.
More time she spends criticizing herself
than priding in the beauty she creates.
Does she not know that her any decision
enchants the breath of the Beach?
Her touch, more than anyone's,
weighs a heaping Heart's cup to spill overwhelmingly,
defines the tropic majesty above the Sun, transcendently.

My Feelings For You
by Alissa Hall

My feelings for you didn't grow because I thought you were "cute",
they grew because I loved seeing you every day
and wondering if it would play out the way I wanted it to.
I fell for your imperfections that were imperfectly perfect.
I loved how your face lit up when you got excited about little things.
I fell for the way you looked at me with those dark brown eyes
that made me feel safe and warm. I fell for every single piece of you.
But after a while your eyes didn't light up,
we didn't talk anymore, and our conversations became dull.
You preferred to post to your social media and hang out with your friends
rather than talking to me and making plans.
I guess everything you said that night wasn't true.
I guess when you talked so strongly about your feelings for me
they were not so strong at all.
Maybe you just wanted attention until you didn't need it anymore.
Or maybe I made you feel better about yourself.
You didn't care about my feelings or how you made me feel.
I guess my feelings for you were different than your feelings for me.

Rise
by Sophie Howe

When She rose, the tide did as well
and She left the water sending ripples to the shore
telling of Her greatness
She is found in every valley,
and strung around your neck
but She won't stay long enough
to let you see Her
She wakes the world with Her voice,
the rushing of the wind, the tapping of the writing desk
the pitter-patter of little feet rushing to their mothers
and She weeps for those She loves
sending storms and sorrows with Her
and She will hold you when you have nowhere left to wander
Her mouth opens wide, Her lips parted to let the flowers grow
and closed harshly when the cold is too much to weather
but She will never be gone too long
for who would pluck the mangoes from the branches
and plant seedling from Her toes?

Idi Amin
by Andreena Johnson-Hall

Born between the years of 1925 to 1927
He was definitely not an angel sent from Heaven
He declared himself to be president
Within his first 8 years, he killed 30,000 residents
In 1979, his reign of terror came to an end
I could only assume Uganda was happy again
He was never brought to justice for his heinous crimes
Which is sad because those people went through a terrible time
In February 1966, which was awhile ago
Amin was accused of smuggling gold from Congo
A few years and 2 failed assassination attempts later
Obote thought about it and declared Amin a traitor
Amin took offense and thought on it for awhile
He decided to seize control and force Obote into exile
Over time Amin lost all his allies
By this time he breaks down and cries
Well this is the end of my poem, I hope you enjoyed
From 1979 to forever, Idi Amin will be eternally unemployed

Repetitive Love
by Dominic Gartner

Oh so repeated, how can such a powerful word lose its meaning?
Even true love can give you a headache.
Just thinking of the word "love", can make one's hand shake.
Yet, in my head, the wound won't stop bleeding.
Even true love can give you a headache.
The second my life got better, I thought my life was stellar.
Yet, in my head, the wound won't stop bleeding.
Nobody seems to believe in Him until they struggle and start pleading.
The second my life got better, I thought my life was stellar.
So many people turn away from everything, for one thing, they misperceive.
Nobody seems to believe in Him until they struggle and start pleading.
It hurts watching the people you love keep making the same mistakes.
So many people turn away from everything, for one thing, they misperceive.
Every day I see someone lose friends or family for what they think is "love".
It hurts watching the people you love keep making the same mistakes.
This repeated word will never go away though; we need to learn to understand it.

Where I Stood
by Marissa McConnell

Hearing the melodies and harmonies throughout the night from where I stood,
I was pulled outside by the haunting grim voice and that is where I stood.
Sitting on the oversized bed too big for someone who didn't have someone else,
feeling like being burned, I jumped off looking over where I stood.
On a park bench, burying my feet into the sand, looking over the shining lake
by the slides, I think back to being a child and standing where I stood.
I stare out the window, the curtains waving from the wind, wanting to be like a bird,
flying into the clouds and feeling the breeze instead of where I stood.
I was surrounded by the broken pieces that you had left behind, scared to move
away, I cried trying not to bleed, furious that you couldn't be where I stood.
Walking away from all my misfortunes, looking for ways to be perfect,
even though I knew that it isn't possible, I look at my reflection where I stood.
I stand by the brick wall, with a curious look not making conversation with anybody
watching how people can fake their smile and laugh where I stood.
I glare at the pictures on the wall from when being happy was easy, reminded how
I used to smile, I remember that being a child is not as stressful as where I stood.
I was separated from the other kids not knowing what I did wrong, I was afraid
not knowing what to do, but I guess I was made to be alone where I stood.
I laughed, finally filled with serenity after the fire went out, no longer looking
at the pictures with disdain, I was hanging by a thread, but I am where I stood.

Montana
by Braeden Sibert

The western meadowlark is the state bird.
It can be found in the International State Park
First inhabitants of Montana were the Plains Indians.
Indians like to take the state animal's hide, the grizzly bear.
Glacier Park has 250 lakes.
You can find the largest migratory elk herd there.
Montana has the largest population of trumpeter swans
In 1888, Helena had the most millionaires
Notorious outlaw Henry Plummer also built the first jail
He might even come from Miles City, Cowboy Capital.
Fishtail City is named after Mr. Fishtail
There's no fish in Glacier Park
The bitterroot is the state flower
It can also be found at the highest point, 12,799 ft.
Montana is also the treasure state.
Fife is named after the wheat grown in Montana

1073 The Force Team
by Emily Mitchell

To think about my robotics team
is to think about a ridiculous thing.
With Integration, Electrical, Mechanical,
BACS, Software, and the CEOS too
all wonderful people who I'll never bid adieu.
Funny moments and sweet memories
with different hobbies and similar dreams.
To laugh with a team, to explore the world
to have adventure on a planet so curled.
Trips on a bus with many colorful people
and by colorful, I mean their language.
The mentors are nice, some funny, some strict
some like an older cousin you wish exists.
I love my team,
I honestly really do.
Thank you for build season 2017
I love you.

Maintenant
by Rebecca Hotz

Every moment is the last of its kind.
A glimmering, gleaming thing, fading to memory.
Now is not forever, not even for a time.
Maintenant.
How can I live within such fleeting instances?
The future becomes the present and will become the past.
I'm hurtled along, never stopping, never pausing.
Dans le maintenant.
We are on the same journey, yet not the same path.
Our unified present becomes an individual past.
We, to I. We, to I.
Je suis le maintenant.
Someday, they say, I'll look back,
Fond of this time that won't be this, but then.
I remember fondly, bittersweetly, the present.
J'étais le maintenant.

Empire
by Edward Dreyer

I look out to the city
all I see is Empire.
I try to flee,
but where can I hide.
All I see is Empire
skyscrapers all around.
But where can I hide
I try to run to others for help.
Skyscrapers all around.
My family is gone.
I try and turn to others for help.
but the others seem to hide.
My family is long gone.
miles away from where I lay.
Others seem to hide
who can I trust to guide my way?

I Sit
by Veronica Johnson

I sit and watch the people around me.
I watch their actions, I watch reactions, I sit.
I sit and observe.
I observe how the nice warm breeze blows by.
I observe the way things move, and the direction the trees brush by.
I sit and I have bubbles now.
I sit and close my tube of liquid fluid.
I notice how there's a little bug.
Stuck in the tube.
I notice how it's slowly plummeting to the bottom.
I sit and relate to the once breathing friend.
I sit and think about how that's me.
About how I feel internally, I was once free and prospering.
Now it's enclosed. Wings damaged.
Life gone. It suffocated.
I sit.

Yellowstone
by Beth Danielowski

As we drove in, rounding those hairpin turns,
My dad was on edge, accustomed to the plains of Minnesota.
I was getting my first real taste of great American mountains,
Charred toothpicks standing on end, shadows of a forest that once was.
We pulled off onto a lookout point, and I peered over the guardrail,
Staring thousands of feet down to the foggy trees below.
How many generations before me had done the same,
Stood in the same spot, astonished?
Along the road was a spring spouting from the stone wall.
My whole life I had dreamt of drinking from the earth.
I ran to the spring and stood in awe.
The faint scent of pine wafted towards me in the cool breeze,
Along with a mist, running its fingers through my short hair.
Looking on, I began my descent onto the stones,
like a pronghorn gripping the side of a cliff.
I stopped on the edge of the spring,
A pane of freshly milled glass.
I dipped my hand in, cupping Adam's Ale.
Its rich mineral taste, forever imprinted on my lips.

The Birthday I Never Wanted
by Taylor Wexler

There I sat in my Clorox scented chair
with many mini monsters all around me.
A tall, gentle man who could see the wild monsters
Through ovals of a piercing object, delivered a message to me.
I never felt comfortable
while listening to the hostile tone that makes my ears cry.
After receiving the terror-stricken news of my travel,
I exited the screeching mass chaos
through the ever so large, brown, wooden rectangle.
My mother appeared in my sight with tear-filled eyes.
She wiped them as if clouds never dropped rain.
She drug me by her frosty, cold hand, not speaking a word.
I am only a young sapling,
who celebrated my birth of 252,455,408 seconds before.
Yet, I did not understand the depressed situation.
How could I comprehend the death of the uncle I barely knew?

Rainbow
by Darryle Aldridge

Purple. Royalty
Kings and queens who sit not on thrones
but stand in crowds throwing rocks and stones
Using their voices to make the silence feel loud
Red. Hot like fire
Anger boils deep inside from years of injustice
A bomb on the brink of explosion, sick and tired of being sick and tired;
they raise their fist not to incite fear but to inspire
Yellow. Things are looking up, so far we have come
A newfound freedom acquired by the power of our tongues.
The battle may be over the but the war is not yet won
Green. Two steps forward and three steps back
A seemingly never-ending field with sharp blades that cut like glass
In times like this we need harmony, brothers and sisters join hands
and walk with one common goal: defeating the enemy
Blue. The only way to go is up.
Pushed down 100 times and yet we stand up 101
Persevere.
We push and push until the gray skies turn clear
Rainbow

Illness
by Caitlyn Althoff

Beginning at youth
My teeth would chit-chatter and my feet pit-patter
I took a sip of water but it felt like being out of breath
And reaching for gasoline
Sitting in a silent room quickly turned to screaming
Sshhh! My head was thinking but it became so loud
Voices talking and talking, I was certain it was about me
The couch I sat on transformed into a shark's ginormous jaw
jabbing at my skin till it pulled me under
Simplistic questions, of "how are you?"
Made my cerebrum overflow with how to respond
Till I said through my teeth, "Fine."
Numbness raked through my body
Unable to comprehend life yet understand everything
People were my enemy and isolation became normal
Outside my sanctuary reeked of burnt flesh
And tasted like formaldehyde
I knew this feeling would soon pass
Yes, I remained in my head.

Moving From Love
by Hannah Sorensen

It's sad to move away from everything you love.
Everything you've known since you were born.
Watching the trees dance and hearing the birds sing,
Every day when you got out of your tiny little bed.
It's hard to move away from everything you love.
Remembering all the birthdays you've celebrated
With all your friends, now you don't know who they are.
Goodbye house. Goodbye friends. So sad I could cry a river.
It's scary to move away from everything you love.
Seeing the Mississippi River as you cross the border,
The water rushing like a waterfall. Get rid of the bad, bring in the new.
It's interesting to move to everything you will love.
Fear is an anchor, let it go.
Spring is in the air, streams of sunlight shining through the clouds,
Smelling the beautiful tulips and daffodils.
It's fun to move to everything you will love.
Harder and harder to hold in your excitement.
Touching all the things you packed in boxes just days before.
Lying in your tiny little bed, the first of many nights to come.
Moving from love is one of the hardest things to do.

More Than Just a Fish
by Olivia Grundman

We dropped the anchor, kerplunk,
A brick shattering a window,
Droplets of water jumping back at us.
The smell of fresh air, a campfire in the distance.
The sky, tainted and painted
With colors of orange, blue, and pink.
Mossy benches, stale and old as time.
Wet feet from the pool of water,
Collected in the bottom of the boat.
Never before, t-shirt weather,
No wind whistling,
Only water ripples and laughter.
A slimy leech looped on my line,
Dancing in the water,
Like a lost string in the wind.
And down it went,
My bobber, notifying me,
Creating too much excitement for our boat.
We make our way back,
Flashlights shining the way,
Returning with more than just a fish.

Mosh Pits, Metal, and Mayhem
by Micah Adams

I entered the venue and heard guitars sounding, drums pounding,
And saw a vocalist running rampant round the small stage.
I heard shouting and smelled the ghastly stench of beer.
I saw people in chairs and people in the crowd thrashing around.
This was a metal show.
I couldn't bear to sit, it was way more fun inside the mosh pit.
I was hit in the face with a smack and I tasted blood.
I was pushed around in a swirling sea of people.
After that I took a break and just watched the bands.
This was a metal show.
I got in line and waited for years for a shirt from the show.
A man as tall as Mount Everest wearing a spiked vest
Shoved me while I was in line so security threw him out.
This was a metal show.
I brought myself to join the middle of the crowd,
As they sang along and threw themselves around.
I couldn't help but smile as I sang.
And I told my father as we started to go
"This was an amazing metal show."

Forget Me (Not)
by Caitlin McDermott

Forget me now,
Forget me not.
Details fade
At the end of the day.
Thinking and dreaming
Are just lost.
Forget me not,
Or forget me now.
I try to hold on
Before it all slips away.
Memories are meant to be forever;
Mine are just temporary.
The past has gone away
In such a blur.
All I can ask,
Is that before it all disappears ...
Don't forget me.

School Is Where I'm Going
by Teagan Coyer

School is where we're going,
Splish, splashing through the glassy rings.
The floodwaters keep creeping up the lawn,
And down my mother's cheeks.
School is where we're going,
The blades of grass are fingers
Grasping at my ankles, they slow my legs from stepping.
The sidewalk is like a twisting snake, beneath the squeak of yellow boots.
A million leaves are staring confident up at me,
through the maple fragranced woods.
But the secret I keep from the leaves and the trees,
Is I'm more scared than a worm from a bird.
School is where we're going,
The building is straight ahead.
The seas of people are gathering now, as dark clouds fill my head.
I say, "The grass won't let go of my feet you see,
we should turn back instead."
I feel the warmth leave my hand when my mother lets go,
she turns and sighs to me, "Don't be afraid of what you don't know,
school is where you go to learn it,
It's an experience you won't ever lose,
and by day's end your smile will be glowing,
So stand up straight, and hurry your boots
Because school is where you're going."

Ever Have You Had
by Jenna Springer

Ever have you been
A flower to the wall
Wander to the back desk
No companion, at all
Ever have you seen
The life of one much better
Off than you could dream
A fantasy, but never
Ever have you had
A conversation complete
You talked, they listened
No, never could you meet
Ever have you lived
Explored the things unknown
Let out a scream of thrill
Just torture, in your home
Ever have you loved
Felt such passion, requited
Long walks, holding hands
In love, you are spited

The Wonders of a Dream
by Velissa Wasfaret

You come to me at night
You bring me such delight
You require of me no participation
Yet you hold me in utmost anticipation
You present to me
A story for only me to see
You fill me with glee
Your enchantment,
Is like an incantation
With you I can do anything;
I can be everything
But when the sky breaks dawn
I find you have gone
Why do you flee?
Won't you stay with me?
I give you my plea
But you must leave
So I wait for thee
To return to me

Heart's Beat
by Maisy Wilcox

the land is everlasting
the ocean and its waves
may levitate the essence
but the essence still remains
and in that essence lingers
a pulmonary glow
an ember of forever
an eternal glimpse at love

Five Thousand Meters To Go
by Amir Ally

Water was my fuel when it came to running.
I could see people relaxing in their chairs as we lined up,
I could feel my shoes hugging my feet tightly,
I took a deep breath.
The smell of fresh cut grass hit me as I jogged up to the cones,
There was a second of serene silence as I started to settle.
"Runners to your mark," the official said, as I prepared myself,
"Get set," continued the official, I was ready.
The gun was as loud as thunder when it went off,
Sounds of shouting were loud in the background as I ran.
My legs felt heavier than bricks,
Green trees, green grass, and the green finish line were all on my mind.

Hues
by Ja'Mel Reed

Throughout our lives we've been made to choose hues
Black or white, pink or blue
But because I wouldn't allow them to make me choose
I was ostracized, I was ridiculed
When faced with the choice
I followed my own voice
Neither black or white, but all shades of grey
Their words and actions would not make me sway
Pink, is what they tried to make me choose
but I couldn't because I only loved blue
Life took its course
but it was me they couldn't force
Because allowing them to choose
would make me lose
Myself

My Passion
by Evan James

My life revolves around one game
That one game can bring me fame
I've practiced for years
Throughout the years I've overcome my fear
It has come above all my friends
It's caused some friendships to end
But I don't know what I would say
About my life if I didn't play
It would be a blank wall
Because my life revolves around a soccer ball

Love Yourself
by Taiylor Baumgardner

Confidence is not my biggest strength
I always tend to keep people at length
"Love yourself," they always preach,
But that's a goal I fail to reach.
I don't look like those magazines,
Those pages full of beauty queens.
They say, "It's okay to be how you are,"
But then they joke on me from afar.
And I always let their words get to me,
With those things they say, I can't not agree.

Growing
by Sara Windoloski

As the winter thaws,
I stand in awe
Watching the once dormant trees
Make way for bird calls.
Spring has officially sprung
We begin to see the sun.
My senior year is ending,
Just as soon as it had begun.
Prom, pictures, graduation
I'll surely receive a standing ovation.
Friends, family, the familiar
Gone once I go to my new destination.
Where did the time go?
What happened to slow?
Who am I supposed to be?
Just wait, you'll see.

Trigger Thumb
by Keil Urban

The chair where I lay engulfed me,
As did the room with the man dressed in white
Waiting patiently in an endeavor to understand.
My mother observing me as a hawk watches its prey.
Sounds of soft, soothing music making me calm
The man knows what awaits, "drink"
He sets a cup, smelling of sweet berry in my palm,
The liquid inside bitter as it runs down my throat
Darkness hisses, a snake leaps at me without warning,
I awake as quickly as I had fallen asleep.
My thumb numb, but moves freely
Finally able to extend.
Now thankful, now know, now older
Now my thumb, finally normal

Those Days
by Makayla Bauer

We used to sit on your gloomy, glum, gray couch
Eating tons of sweet pink ice cream.
Looking back at those exciting days always made me smile,
I miss the days where you took us on breathtaking adventures,
The animals would sing and laugh
as we walked through the bright green forest,
I miss the days where I could see you shine with happiness,
Your smile radiated bright as the morning sun,
Soon those days went away,
It became harder and harder to hear your voice,
Harder and harder to see your happiness shine,
When the news finally came that you drifted away
like a dry leaf in the wind
I couldn't help but taste the ocean waves streaming from my eyes.
The worst part about you drifting away came days later,
Like the aftermath of a tornado,
Looking down at your lifeless pale body
As you lay in that cold metal casket
With the earthy aroma of red roses saturating the air.
As time and time passed
The feelings of heartbreak and restlessness went away.
Soon my sad wilted flower of a heart bloomed again
never being able to forget those days.

Five Years Ago
by Thomas Stockett

Five years ago, I cared so much
I cared what people thought of me
Five years ago, I cared so much
I cared when I got teased about my glasses
Five years ago, I cared so much
that I changed my look
Five years ago, I cared so much
that I tried to be cool like everyone else
Five years ago, I cared so much
I'm glad I don't care anymore

Our Colorless World
by Elizabeth Ellister

The moment we first open our eyes, we see a colorful world.
A colorful world filled with a plethora of vibrant hues,
radiating vitality from every pore.
Fragrances that trigger euphoria from scent alone,
drifting through the breeze.
Melodies, dancing at the passing of dusk,
and singing to the coming of dawn.
Potent flavors that vie for dominance over eager tongues.
And touches that prickle the nerves,
causing shivers of elation to ripple throughout wanting vessels.
The shining brilliance of these sensations clash
and engulf one another like raging storms of incredible intensity.
So powerful, so inspiring, so captivating, so ... Full of life.
Then ... It's gone.
In its place, a gaping hole of addiction.
And memories of longing to entertain the dreary days.
The label assigned to the realm that houses this addiction is boredom.
Shades of grey permeate the realm's exterior.
Previous stimuli that galvanized feeling
now dulled by the vacancy of what once was, leaving ennui in its wake.
We struggle to find substitutes in the static that is ones and zeros,
the ink drawn on decrepit pine paper, the release that drugs provide
and the boiling adrenaline that anger and fear lavish us with.
But the craving for our lost fantasy never truly abates, only smolders,
the whispers of positivity that brush our consciousness
only ever holding it at bay, for a time.
This eternal struggle defines us
and is the film in which we interpret our world.
Our colorless world.

Faith
by Benjamin Kane

As I listen to you slumber I think to myself, "Is she dreaming of me?"
The thought that your breath will forever be my lullaby
puts me at ease as I say my goodnight.
I'll be with you tomorrow
And every day after that,
beginning the transition as I drift off to your soft, gentle lullaby.

How To Love Her
by Samuel Malesky

Love, romance, unique and individual to the slightest bend,
you don't learn the tricks to love, and perhaps that's where we all go wrong-
we try to love someone the way we loved another
In the way we are all different from each other, so must be the way we love
If you find someone new, don't love them the same old way,
but adapt and learn and love her a new way- become her student!
Not so that you might know everything to know about her,
but to show her she is a topic worth studying
Show her you know she's unlike anything that has or ever will be again
acknowledge her differences and adjust accordingly!
Don't send her roses if she likes tulips,
don't send her tulips if she likes daisies,
don't send her daisies if she likes daffodils-
show her you pay attention to detail
and you aren't drawing parallels with past lovers
Chase her and what makes her, her
Don't however, try to capture her heart, let her be free
to come and go as she pleases- after all you fell in love with her heart
when it was unrestricted in the first place;
her individuality is just as important as her time spent with you
Allow her to grow and find herself, and if it just so happens
it isn't with you then so be it,
but don't allow the influence of others change how you love her
Love is natural and fluid, romance is authentic, you don't "make the mood"
Romance isn't manufactured, allow love to grow organically,
and romance to develop on its own, be genuine in your interactions,
and heartfelt in your responses, never stop chasing the sense of wonder
you feel in the initial weeks of a relationship,
be your own person and allow her to be too,
find something new about her to fall in love with each and every day
Relationships are destroyed when the sense of adventure
and exploration is gone, when you've decided you don't love her for her
How to love her you ask? The way she was always meant to be

Less Is More
by Rose Bauer

We always give ourselves less;
Less waking to the blues
That jump through the rays,
Less recognition to ourselves
When we get up every day.
We give ourselves the messes,
Where others come out unscathed,
And us, scraped and bruised
From every bump in our paths.
But what we find is happiness,
Through the thunder in the sky,
And the small glittering droplets
That appear in a cry.
Nonetheless,
We only believed to express
That we didn't need anything at all,
Because we acknowledged our climb
More than we did our fall.

A Rant
by YaTing Chen

A rant is a battle of persuasion
That dictates reason and logic
Firmly, passionately
Unwavering.
It's like a sprout of fire
Innocuous, submissive, puny
Underestimated
Until the fierce blaze
Licking at every junction
Dissolves from numbness into adrenaline
Boiling over, a flood of words
Nourishing the wallflower
That dares to preach
Confidently, stupendously.
A rant is a metamorphosis
That molds musings into ideals
Magnificently, graciously
Undeniable.

A Fake Break
by Lauren Cunningham

I had angered my parents
Listening was not my plan
I could smell the tension in the room
Like a geyser about to erupt
Ow! Ow! Ow!
Dragged to my room I went
It didn't bring me pain
But they didn't know that
Which arm was "broken"?
I could not recall
My parents could never forget
Eyes filling with tears
As I lie on my bed like it is my best friend
The gig was up

Hiss
by Nicholas Cowden

Traveling all day
cramped dining car
hiss
you have arrived
Down the highway, 75 miles per hour
hiss
of course your tire found that shard of glass
Afternoon luncheon,
cucumber sandwiches, cake, scones
hiss
the tea is ready
Climbing up the mountain
perspiration flows down your back and brow
hiss
you scream, it slithers away
Luxury to perspire, you feel the steam
hiss
you enter the Turkish Bath
Cool rain pours down on the hot desert lake
hiss
the needed storm is here

October 26th
by Amanda Lavender

I stumbled into the room, bleary-eyed-- there she lay
Five months ago it happened
The dreaded diagnosis escaped the threshold of the doctor's lips
And there we sat-- breathless
And now, the greyish fog taints her skin
And her head-- permanently exposed, permanently desolate
I attempt to speak a worthy farewell,
But all that escapes are anguished tears
Her heart a thief of her lungs' lifeline
Deafening, laborious breaths seep out of motionless lips
Her pulse drops, drops, drops,
And then all at once-- it stops.
Her soul sinks into an endless abyss,
Yet strangely, so strangely, she appears at peace again,
Her flame is extinguished.

Drowning In a Sea of Sadness
by Jessie Perez

I'm slowly fading away
Remembering the memories we shared together
Without you here I don't want to see another day
My dearest, our love will last forever
Staring out into the space
Your name is engraved in my veins
I have no one here to share this pain
My chest now feels so hollow
Making your passing hard for me to swallow
Just like the pills some people take
I know my heart has begun to break
The tears from my eyes couldn't fill a lake
Not even the seven oceans could be filled
I try to remain calm and sit still
But how can I, when I just lost the one I love?
I cannot help but to wish I could see you again
Just to have one last moment with you
I just hope that you're in a better place
I will run away and leave no trace
And I'm drowning in a sea of sadness

A Memory
by Kayla Owens

A babbling reminder of what was and now is
Of what used to be and is still
Place of visions which linger in the temporal lobe
A simple act controlling an infinite number of emotions
Operating like a system
A cycle of thoughts
Storing the most important things
A machine which never crashes
You are the operator
A tour guide of one's own ideas
Without it you will be lost
A series of explanations will be considered
Scenarios of disorders and troubled pasts
A blankness if ever asked about
Only you can see it
A desperation for remembrance
Don't lose it
A recognition of what is seen
Don't blink
A memory

Silent Tears
by Rachel Page

How many times have I left,
Walked up the stairs, and sat on my bed?
How many times have I stared at the wall,
Not doing anything, just sitting?
How many times have I thought 'I can't'?
I sit, alone, as the tears slide down my face.
I sit, in silence, as my body shakes.
How many times have I sat like that?
And how many times have I gotten up,
And gone back to my family,
And have them not notice my tear-stained cheeks?
How can they not notice?
They say that they love me– shouldn't they notice?
How can I feel so alone among people who care?
I go back to my room and sit down again.
I curl up, hugging myself, as tears stain my pillow.
How many times have I cried those silent tears?

Sinking To the Bitter, Cold Depths
by Sarah Sechtman

Barbells for limbs, weights for joints
Concrete skin with iron nerves
Glassy eyes and unwilling ears
Leaden blocks dragging the ground
Poison arrows flinging through space
Murderous scenes sticking in minds
Wiry walls hiding the faces
Fraying ropes binding opinions and beliefs
Rusting chains pulling hearts and souls
Crumbling bands trapping courage and nerves
Slicing cuffs blocking actions and deeds
Loosening gags absorbing desires and pleas
Made from concrete and metal, weights and chains
Weapons and walls, and ropes and gags
So much weight, sinking deep down
Too much restraints, flailing in vain
Shed the metal and drop the weights
Rid the scenes and break the walls
Slip the ropes and snap the chains
And finally rise above the waves

Apathetic Ambition
by Ian IrizarryNegron

I'm staring at a cloudy sky; I gaze upon a tree.
Its branches how they reach so high, as if to rival me.
The tree knows I am not as close to feeling Heaven's touch.
The tree knows I cannot obtain the light beyond its brush.
How beautiful a bright white bird then lands upon a branch.
It chirps away with stick in claw and adds it to its stash.
It makes a nest and lays its eggs and then it sits and rests.
And as it does the hiding sun keeps moving to the west.
I take an axe; I raise it high; and strike with all my might.
With every strike I chip away a portion of its height.
The tree then shakes; the bird awakes; with fear it flies away
The tree then falls; it once was tall; now on the ground it lays.
Triumphantly I stand upon the carcass of my foe.
The light it blocked; the life it housed; it's under my control.
But then I hear the white bird chirp as it flies high above.
I watch it as it passes by; defiant is the dove.
Where will it go now that its home has been destroyed? Let's see!
I take my axe and follow close; oh look!! Another tree!!

A Façade Among Us
by Davina Applewhite

There's a façade among us
they'll come to find out,
though they see nothing but smiles
Through the pain and the terror
our lips are turned upwards
despite the tribulations and trials
Our complaints go unnoticed,
our worries, unheard
then we become another file
Of "I should've listened,
I should've noticed
the storm brewing in my own child"

The Obvious Mystery
by Isaac Ringold

If you look into my eyes, you can see something much deeper
Maybe a soul inside of a body that isn't supposed to be here
But with these eyes you would think that everything would be clear
And with these eyes you would think that everyone would be a seeker
I know the feeling of hate and love, disbelief and trust
I am a human being, as we all are made of stardust
I have a feeling something bigger than this planet will come to us
Possibly another dimension with our reflection looking back at us
We think that people will change,
and we think that people will stay the same
Some people think that life is just a game, and they might be right
Some people think of what it's like to die, all day and night
We think that most people are rude and they're the ones to blame
For many years now we've been seeking for another planet
that can sustain human life
Because we know Earth will be destroyed by a great ball of gas we call light
Sometimes I wish humans didn't exist because then Earth would be all right
Sometimes I think we can do something better, something nice
I know what I have said, I am always in my mind
I know that these prescription drugs can kill you from inside
Nobody really knows what lies on the plane of the afterlife
If you look into my eyes, you can see I am not blind

Love Did Not Exist 'Til This
by Rebecca Madsen

Dear lover,
Life is given for one to love another
and my life was meant to love you, forever.
Memories of running in meadows and utter bliss,
dances under the stars and a stolen kiss.
Love did not exist 'til this.
Purer than the moon,
even the stars did gaze back in wonder.
And the sun did not feel the need
to outshine my bright angel.
Love did not exist 'til this.
If ever two were meant as one,
it is me and it is you.
Love did not exist 'til this.
One final kiss as we say goodbye.
Death has come for you, but when you die
I shall not love any other
and instead wait
until I join you in the ever after.

Moving On
by Nyah Maurer

"Are you ready to go?"
"I think so."
Leaving everything I know:
the apple tree,
the wire fence,
the woodburning fireplace.
At 5 years old, I never cared much for that house,
but I never thought I'd have to leave.
My mouth was dry and heartbeat loud,
but I never felt tears come to my eyes.
Whoosh! I flung the dazed door open.
The smell of paint flooded the house.
The house was vast and vacant.
I sprinted up the velvety stairs to discover more.
I adored the bedroom with two monstrous windows,
looking upon a new neighborhood as big as a new universe.
I was a princess in a castle, ready to relish my kingdom.

I'm Amanda
by Jamie Duncan

Slowly sipping on the shimmering soda.
Cooling myself down from the harsh outside weather
that feels like a scorching desert.
Placing the smooth plastic cup on the brown side table next to the couch
Then I pulled myself up onto the lumpy sofa.
While observing the daycare,
I hear the other children screaming and playing.
The smell of cinnamon invades the room
and the only light allowing me to see
is coming from the thousands of windows throughout the room.
A blonde girl snapped my attention from the others
as she leaped up onto the couch as well.
She had ocean blue eyes, round cheeks, and goddess blonde hair.
We sat there in silence until she said,
"I'm Amanda"
She instantly became my first friend,
And soon after, my best friend.

Halloween
by Jordan Hagen

Last year, October decided not to end.
I became a vampire, hiding from the sunlight,
Living like a werewolf, only coming out
when under the protection of the moon.
Halloween has gotten old.
I became a pale ghost, searching for centuries
for closure I could never find,
Moaning and groaning like a zombie,
Exhausted after any amount of work.
Halloween has gotten old.
I became a mummy, hiding behind my bindings
to conceal my stream of salty tears.
My bed was my tomb, and buried by my cold soft sheets
I wasted away my days.
Halloween has gotten old.

The At Bat
by Gavin Renwick

It's my time.
All the attention of the audience
focused on the greatest moment of my life.
My team of boys on the dark pine awaiting the aftermath.
Ready to take a try at the impossible task to be accomplished.
The smooth white of the batter's box puts my stomach on a roller coaster.
Thinking back to all other insignificant at-bats
that could have changed the outcome.
On the bump, a kid hurling the rock like a blazing cannonball
in the heat of battle.
The nervousness of being the zero but the glory of a wet Gatorade shower
is so sweet a taste if the task of a frozen rope to deep center is achieved.
The flag in left field shows doubtful the wind will carry me there.
I close my eyes and swing with all my might.
Crack!

Rose-Tinted Glasses
by Grace Johnson

It's hard to see red flags
Through rose-tinted glasses
Until someone comes up,
Punches you back into reality
And cracks them.
This battlefield is not a gunfight
Nor a land of desert or jungle,
It is inside my head, where you can place
And implant your troops as you please,
All the while, I am unaware.
Barricades, you tear down.
Walls, you crash through.
Until standing at the epicenter of myself,
Your true self begins to peek, as I begin to see what's inside,
waiting to be unleashed,
As you shoot the sandbag walls
That tower around me with an RPG of emotion.
After all the dust and debris has settled,
You glare upon a helpless girl, waving her white flag,
With shattered, bloodied, rose-tinted glasses.

In the Valley
by Austin Getz

Held out my hand just to feel the heat
The fire swells and makes me feel I'm obsolete
I'm a heartbeat away for surpassing as
A doll that's made of tears and broken glass
Fragility doesn't seem to mean a thing
I guess like I dismiss proposed engagement rings
But I still feel their entertainment's lust
So I bled out and they watched it turn to crust
In the valley where we're all bored to death
While we're alive we flirt with love and theft
There's not a thing that you can do or say
It's in the themes of their will and of their way
They can't create because they aren't God
So they just break and suffocate the good they've got

The Moment of Truth
by Grahm Hertaus

The infinite possibilities overwhelmed me,
and my enlarged, eager eyes could not wait another second.
The sun awoke from his slumber.
Delicate flakes of snow descended from the sky,
creating a cover for the ground like a blanket.
I emerged from the safety of heated blankets on my bed.
The bitter cold ran goosebumps throughout my body.
Under my feet, the floorboards made the sound of a million shrieks.
Quickly, I made my way to Taylor's room
to enlighten her of the time of truth.
"Smack!" I accidentally slapped her out of pure excitement.
"What?" she demanded.
With curiosity I asked, "Do you know what awaits downstairs?"
Her anger dissolved faster than salt in water, replaced with a jubilant smile.
We tiptoed downstairs to an extraordinary miracle.
The cookies and milk had vanished
while presents had been delicately placed under the tree.
The fresh scent of the pine-needled tree lured us in.
I picked out my present
and ran my hands against the coarse wrapping paper,
The infinite possibilities overwhelmed me.
I obliterated the wrapping paper and opened the present.
Laying on the inside, the one thing I asked for; a basketball.

Pretty Red
by Casey Jones

A lack of words on pages
A lack of thoughts expressed
And you wonder the reason why I'm still depressed
No one ever cares about me
No one ever will
I will have to stay here until my brains spill
With my pen and paper
And my plenty thoughts at hand
All these thoughts no one will ever understand
I'm broken beyond repair
I'm lost and oh so scared
But no one ever dares
Care for the girl with the pretty red hair

Broken
by Tyler Samion

The air is burning our throats,
feeling as though lava is being poured through our bodies.
Finally after waiting for an eternity the coach frees us from imprisonment
and rewards us with water for our suffering.
Some barely make it to the broken bench while others march on inside.
Dragging ourselves through the door we walk at the pace of zombies,
barely moving a step at a time throughout the dimly lit hallway.
Ahead we see a doorframe with handprints left
from boys showing off their masculinity.
Now halted at the doorframe my friends launched themselves
up to the doorframe, grasping the edge like their lives depended on it.
Waiting behind I smelled the putrid stench of sweat swaying in the air
coming from friends who were now wet dogs.
Disappearing to the oasis of the drinking fountain,
I'm left alone with a doorframe
staring me down asking me, daring me, challenging me.
Jumping up I gripped the throat of the frame as if to strangle it,
But instead I found myself falling.
The feeling of the metal in my hands was gone,
and soon I'm grasping the air.
Smack! I connect with the ground sounding like a colossal twig breaking.
My friends start to walk by asking, "Is everything okay?"
I smile like the last couple seconds were just a myth
and respond, "Yeah, I'm fine!"
Pain flowing through my wrist like rapids on a river.
Unlike water though, I was broken.

A Cry For Help
by Mattea Urbia

Thousands of tears rolled down my face, off my cheek.
I look back to that day and still recall everything.
It was not easy to leave my friends, family, and all my memories, it never is.
The first look into the unfamiliar. The strange. The new.
Busy yet not full of life.
Loud but not cheerful ... look to your right
you see a brown broken billboard as I took my first steps to my new life.
The message was clear, it was as welcoming as purgatory.
All I could hear, car alarms shrieking as if the country was crying for help.
Look your left and you could see mountains, beautiful and full of life
it showed what once was and never can be again.
The smell of the Ávila smelled of fresh dew on a spring morning.
The smell of the city smelled of burning tar and oil like the city itself,
down to its last embers.
As each day passed by I wish I could reach out
and touch my home country again.
This country was not my friend
but I soon came to realize it was its own worst enemy as well.
I fell in love with what would have been.
The culture was pure, the food they made would sizzle on the fire
and tastes fresh and piquancy.
Each new day brought a new adventure.
Strangers became friends and new memories formed.
Every step I took had been a new sight, a new experience.
Each passing day I learned something new
about the city for whom needed help.
Each passing day I learned about the people
who were and still are crying for help.
I sit down on an old broken chair recalling my past
I miss the unfamiliar. The strange. The new.

In Their Eyes
by Jacqueline Bethea

Sometimes I look deep into the eyes of my father.
I see his dark knuckles, tough and tired
I wonder if some days he feels the fire
of the tie wrapped so chokingly 'round his collar
He works his hands on a cut-short salary
in hopes that someday he can retire.
Nightmares of his become nightmares of mine.
I am but his daughter and this too is my strife.
Sometimes I look deep into the eyes of my mother.
The worry-stricken words she utters
I know she thinks about me and my brother
working double-time to catch up with the others
Just as she and her many mothers before her
did to sustain their children's wonder.
Nightmares of hers become nightmares of mine.
I am but her daughter, and this too is my strife.
Sometimes I look deep into the eyes of my brother.
I stopped letting him watch the news because I wonder,
If when he looks in the mirror,
is he smothered by visions of Martin, and Brown, and Garner?
Will reality tear his innocence asunder?
Nightmares of his become nightmares of mine.
I am but his sister and this too is my strife.
A world that's full of struggles unseen,
can make the struggling split at the seams.
I will not cry. I will not falter.
I'll carry on for my mothers and my fathers, and my brothers.
Because nightmares of theirs are nightmares of mine,
And it will take someone who sees injustice to render its fabric redesigned.

The Moonlit Lady
by Marley Jones

Soft amber glowed from a dying candle, coals of black
Illuminated by dancing flames in the fireplace on cold September nights.
As she grew so did the moon, filling the void in her soul
    Where the bright light of night belonged.
    Dying embers reflected across beige skin
    On cushions made of silk while she slept.
Eyes of dreary dreams, vacant holes where the ocean breeze
    Ebbed and flowed, leaving longing.
Her deep gaze could take a man's life, because how could they hope
To stare back at someone so divine without losing their breath?
Surely God had spent much of His time shaping the gentle curve of her hips
Like a coastline snaking along the ocean and tracing the curve of her jaw
    To be as gentle as the caress of a lover.
    Though people said God has no favorites,
When they looked upon her they rendered themselves mistaken,
    For someone who walked so tall, and whose words
Crashed down upon others like a wave upon the roughest rock,
    Must be in good graces with the Creator.
Because why were humans created at all if not to stand in awe of her wake?
    Where she stepped, daisies climbed past the blades of grass
    And reached to the sun. The sun that awakened each day
If only to look upon her. And when she breathed, the very air
That escaped her lungs turned to the sweetest whispers of steam.
    And in the cold winter months, when her breath
    Turned to crisp white smoke, it curled around her lips,
    Yearning to enter once again into her lungs
    Because never had anyone breathed life so flawlessly.
Her body was like a flowing gown, as cold and smooth as the finest silk.
    The fabric draped from her sweet skin
    Like a branch of ivy crawling up the sides of a rain gutter.
When she stepped outside the stars fell from their place in Heaven
    To hail upon her beauty.
And she would reach to them and place them back in the sky
In new constellations of white and gold, in designs that pleased her.
    And when death came to her, she offered a cup of tea,
    For her manners were far above her worry.
And the Grim Reaper, with his cloak of souls and wretched scythe,
Walked her to the door of Heaven as if it was an old acquaintance
    Come to visit. And she, with lips like plump red berries
    And heart as generous as a mother's,
    Bent forward and laid a kiss upon his cheek.
    For had he not made certain her safe travels to Heaven?
    The world cried as she walked away from Earth,
    Leaving a garden of daisies drifting up to the sky.
But although her beauty had stuck to her, like the salt to the sea,
    Her soul was tired. And so she walked towards God,
    And laid down on a bed of silver fur to rest.
Her movements every part as graceful as they had been in her youth.
And the world wept when she left. And the world wept as she left.

My Brother Is a Bird
by Rachel Stec

My brother is a bird
The wind leads him through life
He is mostly concerned about its currents
Constantly surrounded by other little birds, he struggles to get the worm
If only he knew the worm could be his if he tried
He has the potential to soar and lead the flock
Instead, he flies in the back, disrupted by the turbulence of others
He was quick to leave the nest, but didn't necessarily know how to fly
Through perseverance and mistakes, flying became natural
His wings grew strong and his mind learned the way
In love with the rush, he refused to come down
But then rough winds knocked him out of the sky one day
His minuscule chirps went unheard and his wings stiffened up
Discouraged by the threat of stormy weather, he refused to take flight again
Despite this, the flock believes that he will fly great distances some day
But first, he has to spread his wings and try

Running
by Cecilia Innis

I've run to the end of some precipice. I've hit a break in my madness
for I can feel the thoughts pressing against my skull.
This constant flow of stimulation to my mind is overwhelming
and I'm falling off a cliff.
Something's crawling around inside of me, driving me over the edge.
I'm running out of feelings, out of creativity, out of sense
because there's no more room for life between the folds of my crazy.
I once had an acute understanding of survival in the merciless wilderness
that is my brain, but I've lost control of all apprehension.
As much as I run from my deafening thoughts,
I'm running out of space for sanity.
Time runs along also, threatening me with its scarcity.
It sneers with each slow, agonizing tick.
It reminds me that my lucidity is of no consequence to its impending agenda.
Yet on I run, twigs and leaves crunching beneath me, legs surging with acid
until there's only a numbness left and my thoughts aren't screaming.
But I reach an end, a precipice,
a break
in the world that reawakens my lunacy.
Oh how I'm running out of space. I'm running out of space in my head.

The Missionary
by Marielle Carpentier

She walks along the path.
Dirt. Sweat. Trash.
The oppressive sun beats down
Her shoes are old and worn-
She walks along the path.
A child rests on her hip.
Five more walk close behind,
with bare and calloused feet.-
She walks along the path,
and hums a simple tune.
the child she holds is smiling,
as the others sing along.-
She walks along the path,
with a grin, broad as the sky.
The wind blows her hair,
and rustles her tattered clothes.-
She looks upon the orphans,
dancing in their mirth.
She smiles because she knows,
she's the richest woman on earth.

Warship
by Katherine Engalichev

Below deck, you are bruised insides,
you are oar shafts lending splinters
to a thousand generations of hands.
Warship, make me fight for you.
Break me like a wave.
You are vessel for the plundered hearts of women,
are you sorry, are you flooding underneath?
Your ligaments are iron,
chaining shadow of dark bodies to your
darker body; chaining your purpose
to trade, to commerce, to slave.
You are the silhouette of a past
ignored or fantasized, singing for the pirate-
not the dead beneath his feet. So leave me,
warship leave me, for you are split ribs and fever,
you are the solemn pain in the chest of humanity,
but when I say crime you say duty,
and your lighthouse calls so sweet, whispers
you still have a home here,
warship, bring your prize to me.

It
by Rebecca Funk

It's the sweat on your fingertips as you fidget.
It will hit you at the most random of times.
3 a.m. but you can't sleep because your heart is racing and your head is spinning.
You're in a dense crowd of people,
Yet it will be the one that consumes you.
You are trapped.
Like living in a glass box,
Yet darkness consumes you.
You exist dismally to the side.
In a world moving ever so fast,
You stay still.
It's wanting to talk but feeling like you're being bothersome.
It's "you just worry too much" or "you stress yourself out"
It's feeling like no one will get it so,
You hold it in.
It's trembling, hyperventilating, "irrational" concerns.
"But what if ... ?"
It's the vast stream of tears as it attacks you.
It's panic, no control, the inability to breathe
But yet, it goes unnoticed.

Vacuum Cleaners Are Evil
by Adrienne Dorenkamp

When I was five years old,
I witnessed my two year old brother
Severely injure himself
On accident.
I sat on a couch as he ran around,
Playing.
I grew bored and joined him,
Ran around,
Playing.
Suddenly my baby brother's fragile frame
Ran into a vacuum cleaner.
Blood gushed from his nose like an angry waterfall.
I had to look away and swallow the bitter taste of bile that wanted to rise.
Our mom ran to us to see what was wrong.
She held him in her arms.
My baby brother's wails took us to the ER.
Teeth were knocked out, others shoved out of place.
His jaw, now broken.
All because of a vacuum cleaner.

3rd Place

Trevin Fitzgerald

Sandwich
by Trevin Fitzgerald

Craning my neck around those corners,
My fingers forming a fist around my soft, cloth hoodie strings.
Running through the list over and over, what's left?
The white, fluorescent lights above my head,
Burning my eyes, hotter than the sun.
Hung on my hands, baskets full to the brim
With a loaf of bread, peanut butter, jam and plastic knives.
A gaggle of gangly children pass me by,
Pushing their cart, creaking with
The weight of sweet, sugary, strawberry pastry cakes.
A distraught mother chases in despair.
"No Pop-Tarts!"
Somewhere, the distant beeping of the checkout
Pings as painful as daggers in my ears.
Making my way to the lines, the dreaded lines,
Where everyone is silently judging, a bunch of hawks.
For my purchase is just outside the norm,
A high schooler, bringing home groceries like a soccer mom.
My veins are snakes, my blood is thick and sluggishly pumping.
I just wanted a sandwich.

2nd Place

Gari Eberly

Las Vegas
by Gari Eberly

There's coyotes screeching outside my window,
but the darkness conceals them
and their eyes don't reflect light like I imagined in my head.
Or maybe it's just the Dover boys from down the street
looking for a little excitement to escape this desert limbo.
Maybe they meant something else when they said jackals cry like girls.
A neon glow bathes my room and I look outside and there you are,
standing among the silhouettes of burnt oak trees.
Your form is black and stilted and you fit in perfectly.
I'm surprised you found my house among the other beige bricks.
We blend into the hills. The road between two houses is infinite
and your only company is the petulant heat wave.
The desert swallows all.
Turn the bowls upside-down or there will be dust in them at morning.
I go outside and lie down on the cracked desert earth.
The flimsy screen door slams shut. No coyotes in the night. It is still.
Your cigarette smoke coils upward as you turn over,
exhaling nicotine bliss but leaving thick tar in your lungs.
I say nothing, but curl my nose into your wind-whipped arm.
You're the realest thing in Las Vegas, you say. That isn't saying much.

1st Place

Anushka Shah

Entering the student poetry contest
as a senior in high school,
Anushka's work is rich in imagery,
and a pleasure to read.
We'd like to congratulate
this very talented young author
as we present
this year's Editor's Choice Award-winning submission,
entitled, "August."

Editor's Choice Award

August
by Anushka Shah

We would lie on the blue-tiled kitchen floor on nights
Where the heat, oppressive and heavy,
would sit on our shoulders, knees buckling.
The kitchen floor was far better,
a reviving coolness permeating through our thin nighties.
Sis had eyes like the fawn who nestled close to his mother
in that dewy clearing in the middle of the forest,
where we once spent an afternoon at the pond, skipping stones,
polished ones, the size of my palm.
Lemon drop in her mouth, she spoke of the ink
that had bloomed indigo poppies on her cotton dress last Thursday.
"Say, don't I smell of sun and dust today?"
and in a bathtub full of milk, she would dream of tomorrow.
Cheeks flushed, eyes ablaze, she was intensely soft.
My own cheeks were hollowing, softness slowly intruded by bone.
My hands, the ones that plaited her wind-tousled strands
and clasped her away, like Mama said, from things unseemly,
were lean and rough:
the pad of my right thumb and pointer finger thickened
from gripping my inky voice and destined arithmetic.
Numb vulnerability melting into the tile floor.
Blindly tracing a school of minnows on her knee,
She opened her eyes with a gasp at the vision above.
Sugared tongue, she gazed at the plaster sky.

Index of Authors

A

Aaron, Erica 142
Abrahamson, Jack 26
Adams, Micah 189
Adamson, Lexi 55
Adem, Faaya 107
Aldridge, Darryle 187
Alejandro-Reyes, Y. 48
Ally, Amir 192
Althoff, Caitlyn 188
Amend, Matthew 56
Ames, Savanna 179
Anchell, Savanna 22
Anderson, Lance 69
Anderson, Molly 160
Andrade, Katherine 58
Appelt, Mckenna 12
Applewhite, Davina 202
Arnold, Sophia 50
Ashman, Luke 131
Austin, Drew 41
Avalos Lara, Daniel 124
Azam, Sarah 75

B

Backhausen, Michelle 18
Bae, Michelle 111
Bajula, Armand 50
Balachander, Ananya 56
Bandel, Brandi 161
Bang, Hannah 39
Barbee, Rachel 180
Barnett, Evelyn 41
Baron, Brendan 137
Barrera, Jazlynn 93
Bashir, Anzal 46
Bauer, Abigail 57
Bauer, Makayla 194
Bauer, Rose 197
Baumgardner, Taiylor 193
Beach, Maggie 146
Beasley, Benjamin 179
Beaulieu-Flolo, Aria 104
Bennett, Amaya 145
Benson, Seyi 103
Beranek, Mark 53
Berezovsky, Chaya Dalya 46
Berry, Emma 141
Bethea, Jacqueline 209
Beyer, Margo 38
Bhowansingh, Aaron 41
Blaeser, Aiden 108
Blaine, Eric 103
Blancett, Kelly 148
Blanco, Josue 28
Blume, Tiffini 170
Bobeck, Samantha 24
Boggs, Virginia 16
Boman, Caitlin 114
Bonny, Justin 127
Brewer, Kelsey 142
Briggs, Kaylee 25
Brockman, Olivia 105
Brodeur, Quinlyn 11
Brown, Kayla 171
Buchner, Clara 101
Byers, Zachary 74

C

Cain, Cammi 175
Cain, Erin 138
Caldwell, Nina 166
Callaghan, Shannon 14
Camacho, Sophia 88
Caminiti, Fox 132
Campiti, Grace 130
Cardenas, Josselin 80
Cardwell, Katie 49
Carlson, Ally 80
Carlson, Jenna 33
Caro, Melanie 39
Carpentier, Marielle 212
Carsten, Madison 84
Carter, Maddi 53
Carver, Paige 130
Cayabyab, Rizelle 37
Chalk, Erin 154
Chen, YaTing 197

Index of Authors

Cheon, Hailey 119
Childs, Kayla 60
Chintakunta, Trishika 61
Chodos, Tamar 45
Chowdhury, Tasnia 92
Christiansen, Conner 170
Ciavarri, Chiara 42
Clements, Delaney 36
Clonts, Elise 161
Corbett, Jenna 109
Countryman, Ella 90
Cowden, Nicholas 198
Cox, Colin 13
Coyer, Teagan 190
Cunningham, Lauren 198

D

Dahlstrom, Emily 168
D'Amato, Nick 24
Dancea, Valeria 43
Danielowski, Beth 186
Danielsen, Elaine 124
Dattilo, Sophie 128
Dauphine, Maire 173
Davis, Jacob 179
Del Borrello, Marisa 123
Desilets, Olivia 11
Detjen, Eric 40
Dickey, Danielle 70
Dillon, Alana 55
DiRienzo, Kailee 143
D'mello, Isabel 39
Donegan, Saoirse 48
Donnelly, Sarah 113
Donner, Kyla 75
Dorenkamp, Adrienne 213
Downs, Jacob 88
Dreyer, Edward 185
Duncan, Jamie 204
Dunkleberger, Laura 126
Dunn, Mialyn 34
Dusenka, Frankie 27

E

Earley, Ty 140
Eberly, Gari 215
Eck, Aidan 169
Eldridge, Vivian 110
ElKhatib, Beesan 100
Ellister, Elizabeth 195
Ely, Jackson 127
Engalichev, Katherine 212
Erkenbrack, Rebecca 175
Erlick, Hunter 36
Evans, Mashonica 134

F

Fafard, Isaiah 52
Farmer, Meredith 165
Feick, Jessica 178
Fellows, Solveig 100
Ferguson, Kareena 82
Fiddelke, Anna 51
Finan, Grace 91
Fitzgerald, Trevin 214
Fleck, Chasey 40
Flowers, Mackenzie 59
Flowers, Margaret 12
Forrest, Mitchell 103
Forseen, Titus 177
Forsyth, Victoria 129
Foss, James 45
Foster, Annabelle 168
Freeman, Anna 97
Freeman, William 49
Frewin, Jackson 53
Fritton, Rachel 52
Funk, Rebecca 213

G

Gabbert, Gracie 32
Gale, Kaylee 81
Garofalo, Paul 54
Gartner, Dominic 183
Gaspard, Adrianna 91

Gerads, Paige 96
Gertz, Naomi 153
Getz, Austin 206
Giddings, Adam 172
Gilbertson, Alexis 109
Gillis, Lydia 151
Gindele, Noah 92
Gomes, Gracie 15
Gracias, Isabelle 128
Graham, Kaya 31
Grendahl, Ryan 173
Grewe, Brooke 106
Grundman, Olivia 189
Guardia, McKenzie 33
Gunnufson, Amelia 146

H

Hagen, Jordan 204
Hall, Alissa 181
Hallberg, Marybeth 20
Hall, Natalie 42
Hamilton, Aidan J. 140
Hancock, Michaelah 43
Hanks, Dallas 71
Hansen, Cassidy 174
Hanson, Lucas 10
Hanson, Maddy 78
Hart, Thomas 57
Hashi, Amina 149
Hass, Mallory 150
Hays, Eva 146
Hembree, Meghan 21
Henriquez, Ariana 36
Hentges, Audrey 59
Hernandez Guerrero, B. 54
Hertaus, Grahm 206
Hillman, Laney 51
Hines, Anastasia 68
Hirz, Andie 107
Hoefs, Lane 89
Holmquist, Thomas 23
Holmstrom, Ella 55
Holt, Tessa 94

Index of Authors

Hotz, Rebecca 185
House, Molly 157
Howe, Sophie 182
Husband, Ginger 15

I

Innis, Cecilia 211
IrizarryNegron, Ian 201
Iverson, Kamrin 78

J

Jackson, Ayva 77
Jacobson, Gunnar 52
Jaimes Morales, B. 49
Jain, Krish 32
James, Evan 193
James, JaKayla 138
Janssen, Brody 122
Jauert, Margot 51
Jenkins, Brianna 162
Johnson, Channy 81
Johnson, Christian 104
Johnson, Grace 205
Johnson-Hall, A. 182
Johnson, Clarence IV 28
Johnson, Jacob 43
Johnson, Leah 106
Johnson, Tiffany 72
Johnson, Veronica 186
Johns, Rowan 115
Johnston, Layton 73
Jones, Casey 207
Jones, Marley 210
Jones, Rosemarie 46
Jones, Sophie 20
Jordan Lopez, Jason 56
Jutton, Erika 164

K

Kamara, Mary 177
Kane, Benjamin 196
Kempe, Josh 99

Kennedy, Makayla 141
Kent, Savannah 74
Kerr, MacKenzie 147
Kett, Klara 29
Kiniry, Madison 86
Kinnahan, Mason 22
Kipp, Jordan 102
Kircher, Hailey 71
Kistler, Peter 181
Kluth, Stella 139
Knoell, Madeline 37
Koberlein, Emily 126
Kolle, Ezra 176
Kommu, Priya 112
Kopp, Genevieve 85
Koranda, Jack 69
Krause, Robert 35
Krupa, John 31
Kugel, Eric 38
Kurban, Hemze 37

L

Lacko, Natalie 29
Lambert, Makenzie 47
Lampton, Brooke 145
Lane-Outlaw, Amelia 58
Larson, Kylie 79
Larson, LaKeysha 114
Larson, Quinci 73
LaTour, Riki 77
Laudo, Joseph 132
Lavan, Grace 38
Lavender, Amanda 199
Lawson, Brie 13
LeBlanc, Julia 87
Lee, Dohee 89
Lee, Lauren 91
Lee, Soeun 87
Leners, Molly 113
Lloyd, Nya 123
Lopez, Alexa 142
Louk, Hayden 11
Lowe, Catie 83

Ludwig, Ellie 90
Luebke, Grace 15
Lunde, MJ 77
Lunzer, Zoë 17
Ly, Hailey 51

M

Madsen, Rebecca 203
Mahler, Natalie 144
Malesky, Samuel 196
Malone, Olivia 144
Maltese, Avery 58
Manni, Brianna 136
Masters, Paryn 162
Matthiesen, Grace 68
Maurer, Nyah 203
Mauser, Taylor 85
May, Samantha 108
Mazwan, Muhammad 34
McCabe, Anna 153
McCabe, Maggie 26
McCay, Maddie 111
McClanahan, Brianna 88
McClelland, Anna 90
McConnell, Marissa 183
McCoy, Taylor 72
McCracken, Mackenzie 122
McDaniel-Neff, Max 166
McDermott, Caitlin 190
McGushin, Katie 125
McHenry, Brady 53
McMullin, Margaret 94
Meeks, Kayla 83
Meeks, Tiffany 174
Mejia Climaco, Nataly 25
Melanson, Andrew 89
Melara, Denis 93
Melvin, Jade 33
Mera Morocho, Giseld 47
Meuleners, Jade 10
Michel, Margaret 167
Miller, Hayden 23
Mills, Henley 14

Index of Authors

Milner, Katherine 155
Mitchell, Emily 184
Mitrenga, Josh 163
Monson, Gabe 10
Montanus, Ella 44
Moore, Mary 95
Moorman, Talya 22
Murphy, Michelle 28
Murray, Eva 40

N

Nephew, Alex 27
Nephew, Mae 76
Nicklay, Hannah 57
Nolasco, Erik 54

O

Ober, Zakkary 33
Oliff, Madeline 72
Olson, Blaine 169
Olson, Cooper 85
O'Neill, Regan 98
Ott, Gabby 178
Owens, Kayla 200

P

Paal, Madison 79
Page, Rachel 200
Paquette, Abbi 34
Paredes-Tinoco, M. 32
Parkin, Makayla 136
Patil, Riya 48
Patrock, Nicole 117
Pavon Peralta, Jennie 73
Payes, Matthew 19
Payne, Liv 16
Pearson, Heather 139
Perez, Jessie 199
Perez, Vanessa 130
Pesek, Cooper 27
Peterman, Brielle 81
Peterson, Margot 21

Petron, Samantha 40
Pevestorf, Nadia 42
Pfeifer, Alleathea 101
Pfeifer, Greta 151
Pierson, Kelby 40
Pineda-Salas, Natalie 102
Poe, Aidan 31
Powell, Julian 138
Powers, Abby 66
Price, Shakara 176
Prins, Kathryn 67
Prins, Kaylee 105

Q

Quinn, Holland G.W. 135
Quinteros, Ariana 51
Quirk, Victoria 22

R

Raboin, Sean 32
Radman, Ashley 66
Ramnarain, Finn 63
Rasner, Karina 92
Redning, Kathryn 70
Reed, Cooper 149
Reed, Ja'Mel 192
Reese, Alana 50
Refsell, Ben 52
Regan, Sienna 18
Reininger, Jacob 82
Remer, Landyn 29
Renner, Dalton 178
Renwick, Gavin 205
Ringold, Isaac 202
Roberts, Keana 131
Rodriguez, Isabella 99
Ronci, Ella 41
Roscher, Maggie 71
Rossen, Sophia 149
Rousseau, Ava 25
Ryder, Samantha 96

S

Samion, Tyler 207
Sanchez, Lizeth 27
Sargent, Sean 30
Saunders, Mikaylah 125
Saurer, Riplee 36
Saylor, Brianna 161
Schaner, Colleen 93
Schmidt, Amelia 136
Schroer, Alexis 76
Schumacher, Rhea 171
Sechtman, Sarah 201
Seeley, Abby 14
Shah, Anushka 217
Shane, Bennett 180
Shea, Katelynn 129
Shupe, Hannah 152
Sibert, Braeden 184
Simon, Renay 50
Skalsky, Gracie 30
Skrukrud, Madeline 164
Smith, Alice 24
Smith, Amelia 76
Smith, Brandy 104
Smith, Rylee 147
Sorensen, Ellie 84
Sorensen, Hannah 188
Springer, Jenna 191
Sran, Ella 116
Sran, Shailee 148
Srinivasan, Advitiya 19
Standke, Coral 150
Stankiewicz, Joel 131
Stark, Colton 11
Stec, Rachel 211
Stecyk, Graceanna 44
Stepp, Mackenzie 167
Sterrett, Sabrina 86
Stevens, Josephine 37
Steward, Kathleen 147
Stewart, Abby 48
Stewart, Rachel 133

Index of Authors

Stillwell, Madisen 68
Stockett, Thomas 195
Stone, Ashlyn 31
Stover, Katelyn 167
Stueven, Nick 35

T

Taylor, Anna 135
Taylor, Jadelyn 26
Tennant, Ella 35
Therrien, Ashley 82
Thoemke, Damon 115
Thomas, Atilia 139
Thompson, Sage 143
Thomson, Madelyn 114
Thordson, Brenna 113
Thornton, Owen 95
Toenyan, Alexa 23
Toenyan, Julia 66
Toftum, Jenna 69
Tran, Ngoc 30
Trombly, Jordan 174
Tucker, Iyanna 165
Turner, Hays 143
Turner, Takoda 4

U

Uecker, Erin 83
Uecker, Jolie 84
Undem, Eleanor 17
Underwood, Caleb 41
Urban, Keil 194
Urbia, Mattea 208
Urvig, Dylan 105

V

Valeri, Callie 110
Van Dam, Quentin 67
Van Lith, Teagen 58

Vasquez, Cristina 137
Vazquez, Carlos 145
Vazquez-Silva, Maryjane 47
Vinje, Amarianna 67
Vivone, Moriah 172

W

Wallace, Davion 49
Wasfaret, Velissa 191
Wasfaret, Vincent 175
Wawersik, Sam 50
Webb, Kathryn 134
Wells, Kaitlyn 160
Weon, Tom 98
Wexler, Taylor 187
Wheeler, Kaili 112
Wibbels, Tristen 112
Wiens, Ethan 97
Wiese, Kyler 70
Wiggins, Keshaun 166
Wilcox, Maisy 192
Wills, Gabrielle 80
Wilmer, Ava 18
Wilson, Carter 23
Windoloski, Sara 193
Wold, Jessica 144
Woody, Lauren 19

Y

Yates, Carly 137
Young, Ariana E. 163
Young, Nick 30
Yousef, Ornina 102
Yowell, Nathan 133

Z

Zitzmann, Abby 26

Treasured
Price List

Initial Copy 32.95

Additional Copies 25.00

Please Enclose $7 Shipping/Handling Each Order

Must specify book title and name of student author

Check or Money Order Payable to:

The America Library of Poetry
P.O. Box 978
Houlton, Maine 04730

Please Allow 4-8 Weeks For Delivery

THE AMERICA LIBRARY OF POETRY

www.libraryofpoetry.com

Email: generalinquiries@libraryofpoetry.com